"Joanne Kraft always comes through with 'milk out the nose' humor that is honest, authentic, and even educational! She's one of my favorite writers."

—James N. Watkins
Award-winning author and editor of *Vista*

"Are you a 'captive of activity' or in 'bondage to busyness'? Author Joanne Kraft asks these and other provocative questions in her compelling new book, *Just Too Busy*, in which she shares her family's antidote to the consuming marathon of life—a year-long adventure in togetherness resulting in a renewal of family love, respect, and intimacy. Kraft invites and even challenges readers to consider taking a radical sabbatical of their own. Suggestions, prayers, and real-life examples fill this unique book. You won't want to miss it."

—Karen O'Connor
Author and speaker
Gettin' Old Ain't for Wimps and
Help, Lord! I'm Having a Senior Moment

"If you feel like someone pressed fast-forward on your life, this is the book for you. Joanne Kraft knows what it's like to be overwhelmed and overwrought. With compassion and humor, Joanne walks you through her family's solution to an over-busy life. Even if you don't take a full radical sabbatical, the ideas shared in this book will inspire you to reclaim peace and simplicity in your life."

—Glynnis Whitwer
Editor of *P31 Woman Magazine*

"Joanne Kraft uses humor and grace to point busy moms in a new direction—a direction that leads away from the fast-paced, super-stressful lives many of us lead. This is a must-read for any mom who feels like there has to be more to life than soccer practice and fast food in the minivan. For the first time in a long time, I feel comfortable—no, happy—to say no to busyness and sit back and enjoy my kids, my husband, and my life."

—Erin MacPherson
Author of *The Christian Mama's Guide to Having a Baby*

"I wish I could have read this book when my kids were younger. Joanne Kraft gives overrun parents permission to finally say 'Enough!' With practical, real-world advice and tons of humor, *Just Too Busy* gives a practical approach to reclaiming your family."

Kathi Lipp
Speaker and author
The Husband Project

D0250942

Just Too Busy

TAKING YOUR FAMILY ON A RADICAL SABBATICAL

JOANNE KRAFT

BEACON HILL PRESS
OF KANSAS CITY

Copyright 2011
by Joanne Kraft and Beacon Hill Press of Kansas City

ISBN 978-0-8341-2690-1

Printed in the
United States of America

Cover Design: Lindsey Rohner
Inside Design: Sharon Page

Unless otherwise designated, Scripture quotations are from the *New King James Version* (NKJV). Copyright © 1979, 1980, 1982 Thomas Nelson, Inc. Used by permission.

Scriptures marked NASB are from the *New American Standard Bible*® (NASB®), © copyright The Lockman Foundation 1960, 1962, 1963, 1968, 1971, 1972, 1973, 1975, 1977, 1995.

Scriptures marked NIV are from *The Holy Bible, New International Version*® (NIV®). Copyright © 1973, 1978, 1984 by Biblica, Inc.™ Used by permission of Zondervan. All rights reserved.

Scriptures marked NLT are from the *Holy Bible, New Living Translation* (NLT), copyright © 1996, 2004. Used by permission of Tyndale House Publishers, Inc., Wheaton, IL 60189. All rights reserved.

Library of Congress Cataloging-in-Publication Data

Kraft, Joanne.
    Just too busy: taking your family on a radical sabbatical / Joanne Kraft.
       p. cm.
    Includes bibliographical references (p.   ).
    ISBN 978-0-8341-2609-1 (pbk.)
    1. Mothers—Religious life. 2. Families—Religious life—Christianity. 3. Simplicity—Religious aspects—Christianity. 4. Time management—Religious aspects—Christianity. I. Title.
    BV4527.K69 2011
    248.8'431—dc22

                                                          2011014297

10 9 8 7 6 5 4 3 2 1

DEDICATION

To Paul, for overlooking dust bunnies, gummy tile grout, and two tiny mushrooms; your love and sense of humor carry me.

To my four good and perfect gifts from above, keep God first and the rest is easy. Your dad and I are rooting for you.

ACKNOWLEDGMENTS

My gratitude to Celia Bonino, my best girlfriend and greatest encourager, who clearly saw the author in me long before I did and whose anointed house in the woods became the labor and delivery room for this book. Thank you, friend.

Thanks to Inspire Christian Writers, you cheered on a mom with dishpan hands and a two-page article to see all God could do with this message. You are gifted writers, editors, prayer warriors, and encouragers—the best-kept secret in Christian writing and publishing today.

Thanks to Elizabeth Thompson, who leads the mighty ICW wordsmiths and showed the patience of Job while reading my chapters over and over again; buckle up, my friend, the Lord is using you in big ways.

Thanks to Rachelle Gardner, my agent, personal firefighter, and friend. You always knew just when to fan the flames and just when to put them out. I am so grateful for you.

Thanks to Judi Perry, for your editing support and gifted knowledge of endnotes.

Thanks to Danielle Bergey, if only you were paid per e-mail question. You were such a help to me.

Thanks to faraway friends Tiffany Stuart, Angie Knight, Susan Panzica, Penelope McCowen, and my readers at Blessed <www.OneSoBlessed.com>, your prayers and encouragement were monumental.

Thanks, Dad and Linda. Your prayers launched me into God's plan for my life. I hope every busy mom reading this book will feel your prayers for them too.

Thank you to my Lord and Savior, Jesus Christ, for entrusting this work to me—while listening to every busy-mom whine and whimper, and loving me anyway.

CONTENTS

PART I

Busy

PULLING YOUR RATS FROM THE RACE 1

Just when you thought you were winning the rat race, along come faster rats.

—*Barbara Johnson*[1]

It's no accident you're holding this book in your hands right now. Do you think it's just a coincidence? Sure, you may have been drawn by the snazzy cover and catchy title, but understand this: there is no mistake here. Your life is pretty chaotic right now, isn't it? You are busier than you've ever been, and you know it. You just don't know what to do about it.

We aren't much different, you and me. Not long ago, I was in the bookstore searching for something—anything—to help me get a grip on my chaotic, topsy-turvy life. I couldn't swing my purse without hitting a book for busy moms. *The Busy Mom's Recipe Book —You Can Make a Fourteen Course Meal in Eight Minutes! The Busy Mom's 4.2-Second Devotional Book, How to Change a Flat Tire for Busy Moms.* Sure, there were lots of books that spoke specifically to me, a busy mom. Unfortunately, they all seemed to accept the fact that I was too busy, and I was going to stay too busy.

I needed help from someone who had walked a mile in my tired, worn-out mommy-shoes. Were there survivors in a head-on collision with busyness? Had anyone been declared victor after jousting the insanity of overactivity?

Why was my life moving faster and becoming more difficult? Slow and easy, that's what I wanted. I looked everywhere for it. I found television shows that explained simple ways to decorate my home for Christmas, simple ways to make a delicious pot roast, simple solutions for annoying pet odors, but where were simple solutions for slowing down? How could I get back some of the time that was being stolen? I even bought a magazine with the word *simple* in the title, thinking surely it would have the answer, only to discover that anything I did, no matter how simple, really wasn't. Slowing down was easier said than done.

We were barely hanging on; our family schedules were crazy. I was a daytime zombie in a minivan, shuttling children back and forth from soccer practice to dance lessons and from Girl Scouts to baseball games. My life was a miserable treadmill, and I was running hard and fast. I was out of breath and exhausted, and getting absolutely nowhere.

Each day I was given another twenty-four hours, and each night I couldn't have told you where all the time had gone. As a family, we were doing more than we ever had before, but we were accomplishing much less, and growing farther apart in the process. It was discouraging. A voice in my head screamed, *This isn't what I signed up for!* Busyness was our new normal, and it was time for a change. The solution I received surprised me, and I had no idea it would be considered radical.

Radical. It's a dirty word to some, and most often used in the context of an insult. The definition means to be *excessive, extreme,* and—my favorite—*revolutionary.* If I were to ask you to think of someone radical, who comes to mind? A person in the United States military might imagine a member of the Taliban. An avid hunter sees a vegetarian. A teenager would, no doubt, envision overprotective parents, and those same parents would see their doesn't-think-things-through adolescent. All are living outside of what is deemed by society as normal. All, in one way or another, are radical.

But I was ready to do anything, even if it meant I looked radical. Busy mom or not, I was tired of feeling patronized. I was sick of hearing, "This is just the way it is: *moms are busy.*" Well, no kidding! I get that. I'm a mom. I know what it's like to go years without sleep. Yes, I, too, have thanked Big Bird and Dora the Explorer for babysitting my child for hours on end. I have changed my fair share of stinky diapers while writing out my grocery list and mowing the lawn. I am a mom to four kids. I can carry groceries like a pack mule—with a child on each hip, shopping bags and purse around my neck. I can even serenade my youngest to sleep and still manage to open the front door with my teeth.

This wasn't the busy I needed help with. That kind of busy can't really be helped. Little ones are an insane amount of work. There is no book out there that is going to solve that. The busyness I needed help with came as my children got a little bit older. Once they were able to tie their own shoes, make themselves a bowl of cereal, and go potty without my full attention, things didn't slow down. As a matter of fact, they began to move at warp speed.

I began noticing busyness becoming more accepted among families. I talked with lots of other moms, and we shared our complaints. When I suggested we try to do less, or say *no* more often, the consensus was resignation. They were used to living this way. "That's just the way it is," they'd tell me. I was starting to believe them.

Being the magazinaholic that I am, one of my light-bulb moments came while reading one. I had originally thought I was reading an article titled "Keeping Up with the Joneses." Actually, it was an advertisement for a potato chip. An ad for snacks on-the-go validating the bondage of busyness I was feeling. This is what I read: "Busy parents Lisa and Jeff Jones spend most weeknights shepherding their kids Michael, 13, Jennifer, 6, and Madeline, 9, from school to sports, from sports to music, from music to swimming, which means that for them, healthy, delicious snacks on the go are not just a 'nice to have' but essential."[2]

Did you notice that second line back there? No, not the part about a potato chip being a healthy snack, which is folly in itself, by the way. These parents shepherded their three children most every weeknight, *after school and homework*, from sports to music, from music to swimming. All in one night! Was this ad really supposed to make me think of snacks on-the-go?

I couldn't get past the insanity this family lived every evening. Nothing was mentioned about that. So, it wasn't just me. It seemed the whole wide world was beginning to accept this craziness as a way of life. It was at this very moment that I began to look at our activity as captivity and our busyness as bondage.

I stopped and really listened to the moms I met at the grocery store. The vast majority of them were overwhelmed and physically exhausted, often from self-induced choices. I have yet to hear a mom tell me, "Wow. This week has been amazing! I am busier than I've ever been, and I just love it!" or "I'm exhausted. I ran from home to work, and then rushed the kids from softball to dance lessons, and boy howdy do I feel great!" The common cry of the mothers I know is a feeling of fatigue, overcommitment, and the helpless inability to make a change. I'm not hearing much joy.

There are four moms I run into on a regular basis at my local grocery store. Which one are you? New Mom? Old Mom? Tired Mom? Blue Mom?

New Mom: My little one was up all night. I think she's teething. Please tell me I'll sleep again before she starts college. I haven't showered in days, and my car has become a U-Haul for a traveling circus of toddlers. Can't talk. I'm running late for Kelsey's newborn gymnastics class.

Old Mom: Busy. Busy. Busy. We are so busy. Taylor made the competition field hockey team. Her games are in Brazil three times a month. Matthew made the varsity football team and has practice eighteen hours a day. It's OK, they're having fun! My husband? I haven't seen him since last Tuesday.

Tired Mom: This mom doesn't have time to chat. She is slumped over her shopping cart, mumbling incoherently with her eyes oddly fixed on some unseen object in the distance. She's wearing her son's college sweatshirt backward and hasn't brushed her hair in days.

Blue Mom: The kids are doing great. We don't see them as much as we'd like, but the grandkids are growing like weeds, so they tell me. No, they couldn't make it for Thanksgiving. Ashley was in a soccer tournament. Bob and I paid to have their family portrait stamped on a few thousand local milk cartons. We finally tracked them down at a basketball game last week. I ran up to hug Jacob and the ref called a foul.

I understand their irritation, bitterness, and exhaustion *completely.* The big difference for me is now I know how to get off that nauseating rollercoaster ride. Changes can be made for the better, and lives can be released from the captivity of activity.

Are you feeling in bondage to your busyness? Are you in captivity to your activity? Or have you been beaten down enough to believe this is just how life is? You need to know something: this isn't just how life is. There is freedom from busyness, because sometimes even the good things in life can become the enemy of the best things in life. I love my children, and I have the bad habit of thinking I can make their world perfect. I run off in twenty different directions to make their lives better, when really, I need to stop and open my eyes to all I'm doing, doing, doing, then ask myself: *will this have any eternal value?* I had an experience as a child that reminds me of how important it is to pay attention and open my eyes.

Open Your Eyes

They say I look just like my dad, but Mom still managed to pass on a few traits to her oldest child: green eyes, a love of reading, and the fear of water. Mom had a fear of water she didn't want her children to experience. When I was eight years old, a creaky wooden gate was my portal into Aylen's Swim School. I can still recall opening it to the coconut scent of Hawaiian Tropic suntan lotion and the sounds of splashing children. Each week I stepped through that door, I might as well have been walking the green mile.

I dreaded swimming lessons.

While I rubbed on sunscreen, my mother and little sisters were gathered together with the other parents in the shade of an overhang to watch the lessons.

"Hurry up, Joanne. Your instructor is already talking with your class." My mom gently pushed me in their direction. I wanted to make her proud. She knew my fear of water, especially the deep end of the pool, so I scurried along.

My pretty, tanned, and fully clothed instructor shared, "Today is a big day. Today you will be jumping into the deep end with your float boards and kicking across the whole length of the pool." She smiled as if this were great news. "I won't be in the pool with you. I know you can do this. That's why I'm not even in my swimsuit today."

When my turn came I reluctantly jumped in, still confused as to why this swimming stuff was enjoyable to anyone. With arms stretched out and hanging on to my float board for dear life, I squeezed my eyes shut tight and kicked my eight-year-old legs as hard as I could. Before I jumped in I had already worked out my strategy. Stay close to the pool wall at any cost. If the deep end was scary, the center of the pool was scariest. There was safety and comfort beside the wall because I knew I could reach up and grab the side if I needed to.

After a little while I thought, *Wow. I sure hope my mom is watching me. I'm doing really great at this.* It was at that moment I heard my instructor's voice.

"Joanne, open your eyes! Look around! See where you are!" she shouted.

Opening my eyes, I looked around and discovered I was in the middle of the deepest part of the pool. My trust in the float board was immediately over, and I went under. My instructor shouted something else to me but it didn't matter, I wasn't listening. In front of a summer crowd of parents, siblings, and schoolmates, I panicked and began to drown.

My fully clothed swim teacher jumped in to rescue me. I was met at the edge of the pool by my mother who awkwardly tried to hold my baby sister and throw a towel around me at the same time. I was mortified. And I thought I was doing so well.

Just like the scary part of the pool, busyness can creep up in our lives. The moment we think we have a handle on things, we can go under. It's my turn to ask you to take a deep breath and survey your day-to-day life. The words of my swim instructor seem quite fitting as you read through each chapter and discover ways to journey from busy to blessing.

Open your eyes. Look around. See where you are.

Here would be the perfect opportunity to jump into the radical sabbatical part of the story. But, in order for you to truly share our journey from busy to blessing, I have to let you peek behind the curtain of my overwhelmed life. I'll let you in on a little secret: denial is where it all started for me.

I am excited to walk with you through these pages. I encourage you to open your eyes to the possibilities. Remember, there is nothing written here I haven't experienced myself. And, as much as my colorful cover and catchy title may have drawn you to this place, my prayer is you'll finish this book with much more.

Dear Lord, pry open my eyes. I'm afraid they may be closed. As I read each chapter, give me perfect eyesight to see my life clearly, the strength to be honest with myself, and the courage to make radical changes along the way. In Jesus' name I pray. Amen.

- How busy is your life?
- What did you accomplish today that has eternal value?
- Do you have time for the important things like reading a bedtime story to your little ones, having dinner together as a family, or time alone with your husband?
- If not, why not?

Frustration is not the will of God. There is time to do anything and everything that God wants us to do.

—*Elisabeth Elliot*[3]

A.D.D.— ACTIVITY DENIAL DISORDER

It's not denial. I'm just selective about the reality I accept.

—*Bill Watterson*[1]

Addiction. The word means to have a habitual or compulsive involvement in an activity, or, in my case, *overactivity* that led me straight into the center of a busy-mom hurricane. Busyness is an addiction. I couldn't slow down no matter how hard I tried. If I managed to find a peaceful pause in my day, it felt unnatural, almost uncomfortable. My body was used to 100-miles-an-hour days, high in busyness and high in stress.

Imagine my surprise when I read this quote in a magazine article: "Because the adrenaline rush from stress creates an unconscious 'reward' in the brain, it can become habit-forming," says addiction specialist John Montgomery, Ph.D.[2]

Busyness is stressful, and stress becomes habit-forming.

So, it was true. I wasn't making this up. Like any bad habit, I had to find a way to stop. The realization I was living on a constant habitual stress-filled adrenaline rush came to me one afternoon. A friend of mine, who was extremely health conscious, encouraged me to begin taking a daily vitamin supplement. I respected her wisdom and began taking them. After the first day, I was immediately on the phone with her.

"Hi, Sharon, it's me. Could you please tell me what was in that vitamin? I have been sitting on my couch all afternoon, and I feel like I've fallen down Alice's rabbit hole."

"What in the world are you talking about, Joanne?"

"*Wasted.* That's the first word that comes to mind. Like, I'm much too relaxed. I thought you were a godly woman, Sharon." I teased her, but it was true, I felt like a zombie.

"Joanne, I gave you a vitamin B supplement. That's all you have there. Vitamin B feeds your adrenal glands. If you're living on a regular dose of adrenaline, I'm guessing the supplement gave your adrenals a good helping of support today. That's probably why you feel wasted. I can assure you everything in the capsule is natural—and legal."

Living a life of busyness can easily lead to stress, and stress is something I was apparently becoming accustomed to. But even with this new evidence pointing to my mom-addiction of busyness, like every addict, for the longest time I lived in the land of denial.

Activity Denial Disorder

"I'm too busy?" I repeated my girlfriend's ridiculous accusation out loud. How dare she judge my life! She had no idea what it was like to raise four children. My busyness was under control. I had always prided myself on that one true fact: *I have a handle on everything.* Constant activity is quite normal. And if anyone had the guts to point out the obvious, I considered it an attack, and he or she was soon labeled my enemy.

A doctor would have diagnosed me with "busyness with a secondary disorder of A.D.D.—Activity Denial Disorder." The prognosis was good as long as I treated this disorder by slowing down. But first, I needed to admit I was sick.

Denial is a funny little creature. It finds wicked pleasure in talking all of us busy moms into believing everything is just fine.

"Oh, goodness gracious, Dear," Denial says as it pats your arm to console you, "the problem is definitely not you. It is obviously everyone and everything else!" Denial pretends to be your very best friend, whispering in your ear: "The children just love getting up at 6 A.M. for a soccer game three hours away—for six months of Saturdays." Denial will sometimes manipulate: "If you don't let your daughter try out for choir, everyone will think you are a bad mom." It will stop at nothing to keep you busy: "You are giving your kids the childhood you never had." Denial will even give bad wardrobe advice: "Of course, leg warmers are back in style."

Have you ever suffered from A.D.D.? I have. I still struggle with it. Go ahead and Google *activity denial disorder.* You won't find it. If you were to search Web MD or Wikipedia, you wouldn't pull up one word on this universal epidemic. Yet this disorder wreaks havoc in the lives of millions every day. It is real, my friends, very real. Even sadder, there is no prescription available for sufferers like me.

Here are a few signs and clear symptoms of an A.D.D. sufferer, and I urge you to pay close attention. I must start by telling you this: the first symptom is denial.

Denial is the disbelief in something true and factual. I've heard it said the first step to healing is admitting you have a problem. But if you don't *think* you have a problem, doesn't that mean you don't have one? I had to admit I had a problem. Recognizing my overactivity was the first step at breaking Denial's spell. Busyness doesn't initially come at you with both guns blazing. It is quite a bit sneakier than that. Are you still wondering if you are a tried-and-true busy mom with A.D.D.?

Let's look at the next few symptoms here. Busy moms look like any other mom at first glance, but if you look closely, the signs are apparent. This mom usually has no time to herself, *ever*. On any given day, she feels pulled in twenty different directions. Well-meaning moms with A.D.D. have a huge problem saying no. They tend to be serial-volunteers—the first to raise their hands for anything. They carry the burden of helping into every situation. If you take the time to listen closely, in one week you will hear these words, "Yes, I'd love to be room mom. Not a problem." "Of course, I can make the team banner." "Carpool this week? I can do it." They love their little ones passionately and will sometimes sacrifice their own marriages to give their children the lives they never had. Sadly, this contagious disorder is epidemic.

Denial Exposure

I'd like to share a little secret with you—something most busy moms in denial would never tell you: They are scared to death of being exposed. These beautiful women are exhausted performers on a stage, hoping that all they are doing, doing, doing will one day be worth it. As a recovering A.D.D. mom, I had convinced myself that the busier I was, the more valued I was. Eventually, I learned all the activities I had my children signed up for had almost nothing to do with my worth as a mom.

Have you ever really watched a busy mom doing her thing? She tries her hardest to make everything look just perfect from the outside. But at the most inopportune times, she stumbles and falls flat on her face. Thankfully, I come from a family who loves to laugh, and since I fell on my face too many times to count, laughter soon became the salve for my embarrassing A.D.D. moments.

Denial Brings a Jell-O Salad

After having our fourth baby, we started attending a new church. Even with a brand-new fourth child, I refused to miss a Sunday service. I made sure to come in with the baby under one arm *and* a green Jell-O salad for the weekly potluck tucked under my other arm. My performance experienced a slight hiccup at church that day.

As our pastor was saying his good-byes to our family, he complimented our two-year-old daughter on her pretty dress. "Grace, what a beautiful dress you're wearing today!" he said. Our church family gathered and smiled at the new big sister enjoying the attention, now twirling for dramatic effect—without any underwear. Grace experienced quite the toddler wardrobe malfunction, and my face lost all color.

What, you say? This type of thing isn't exclusive for A.D.D. moms? I would completely agree with you—if the same thing hadn't happened again the following Sunday.

Doing too much was becoming a problem, and denial wasn't helping one bit. Before I could treat this busyness disorder in my life, I had to see it for what it is. Denial may have been my problem, but with it came a side helping of regret.

Denial Plus Regret Equals My Enemies

There are a few fears I battle as a mother: homicidal maniacs, drunk drivers, cancer. But the biggest fear I have by far is *regret*. I hate regret. I want as little of it as possible in my life. It is the one enemy I can almost feel looming in the shadows as my children become older.

If my archenemy was busyness, the commanding officer in his evil army was regret. It was going to take some work, but I planned on being victorious in this battle. You see, I am always up for a challenge. I was raised by a former United States Marine, a man who served three tours in Viet Nam; a man who taught me to never quit. "The fastest way to get you to do something, Joey, is to tell you, 'No, you can't do it.'"

I refused to accept my family's overcommitted existence the way it was. Changes needed to be made. If it meant that our family did things a little bit differently for a while, so be it.

Being a Little Different Is OK

When I was a teenager, I was always the first in the house to wake up. I wanted first dibs on the shower. As the oldest of four children, three of us girls, I had to get up very, very early. C'mon, it took a long time to get that big 80s hair! I should rephrase that. I was the first *kid* in the shower; my dad was the first in the house. My normal routine was to wake up, walk down the hall half asleep, and find my father reading his Bible at our kitchen table. That was his cue to get up, his metal Thermos in one hand and his lunch pail in the other, bend down to give me a quick kiss, and head out the front door. Before he got into his beat-up El Camino, he would do what I remember him doing every morning, he would hang his American flag.

One morning it was raining pretty hard. As Dad fought the weather to put up his fabric friend, he was met by our neighbor Sid, who I spied through our front curtains walking across the street with purpose, a small paper booklet clenched tightly in his hand.

Sid didn't waste time with pleasantries. He walked right up to my dad on our front porch and said, "George, I'm not sure if you know this or not, but it says right here in the official flag-flying handbook that you can't fly the American flag in the rain."

Without pausing, my father finished hanging his flag and turned. Looking Sid in the eye, he said, "Sid, I fought for this flag in the rain, and I am going to fly this flag in the rain."

My dad wasn't going by the rules, and that made quite an impression on me. I was proud of him. I knew taking a radical sabbatical of any kind was going to be considered not playing by the rules too. There were going to be people who looked at us oddly and scratched their heads in confusion. We couldn't let that stop me and my husband from moving forward and trying to change something we felt was broken in our family: we were too busy.

We needed to seriously evaluate our activities. I had a flaming case of A.D.D., except now I was no longer in denial. My habit of busyness had to stop. I didn't enjoy being this busy, and when I took a moment and looked at my children running alongside me, they weren't happy being so busy either. Just another reason I knew things must change.

Time was like a runaway train, and our activities and busyness were the fuel that sent it racing down the track. We were flying right through special moments and precious years we would never be able to get back. My husband and I had been told we couldn't stop time, and no one we knew had ever stopped a runaway train and lived to tell the story. We decided we were willing to do anything to stop it, or we'd jump trying.

When I was no longer in denial about my addiction to busyness, I was much more receptive to seeking ways to slow down. I told myself that one day I'd learn to slow down, but, just like a diet, I put it off for as long as I could.

God's plan for us was a much bigger step than we'd anticipated. But before I share our year-long time out, I want to share my list of ten telltale signs—ten flashing lights—that confirmed I was too busy. You see, even with all of the warnings to slow down, I still wasn't convinced.

Lord, remind me when I'm doing too much. Heal me from this flaming case of A.D.D. Help me see the best ways to use your gift of time and keep the enemies of denial and regret far, far away. In Jesus' name I pray. Amen.

- Are you addicted to busyness?
- Do you think you might be suffering from Activity Denial Disorder?
- When was the last time you fell flat on your face while trying to overachieve?
- Which activity in your busy schedule has eternal rewards?

Let's face it. None of us can do a thousand things to the glory of God. And, in our own vain attempt to do so, we stand the risk of forfeiting a precious thing.

—Beth Moore[3]

TEN TELLTALE SIGNS 3

Beware the barrenness of a busy life.

—*Socrates*[1]

David Letterman is famous for his top ten lists. For decades he's entertained millions of viewers each week with everything from Top Ten Signs You're Not the Most Popular at School to Top Ten Things Never Before Said by a NASCAR Driver. So I decided to sit down and make my own list. A very unscientific list of ten telltale signs I was too busy.

10. It was official. I was a marathon runner.

I hate running. Running in a marathon is an unspoken dream for many women, hours of grueling training, pushing to the point of exhaustion, while focusing on an unseen finish line. No. I don't happen to be one of those women. Oh, I love to cheer on anyone who is dedicated and self-disciplined enough to achieve goals and accomplish his or her dreams. But the idea of running until I'm nauseous, lungs burning, and sweating like a boot camp recruit doesn't appeal too much to me.

26

As much as I detest running, and despise even the mere thought of it, would you believe I'm known for my running excellence? Each morning when I wake up and throw my legs over the side of my bed, someone slaps a paper number on my back, laces up my running shoes, and shoves me into a crowd of ladies who hate running just as much as I do. That someone is me.

From the crack of the starting gun, I'm off. I begin slowly. Pacing myself, I make lunches in the morning for my children. Moments later, my stride still steady, I drop each child off at his or her school destination. Keeping the pace, I run my errands for that day, checking them off my list. This is when I start to feel the burn. I pick up speed when the children get home from school. With homework finished, once again we quickly run out the door. This is where I hit my stride and my children join me in the race.[2]

We sprint together from one after-school activity to the next. Just like you, I love my children and want them to have joy-filled childhoods experiencing team sports, community theater, choir, and football. Those are all part of that joy, aren't they?

9. My kids thought all meals came with a side of fries.

OK, so I may be exaggerating. But only a little. One thing I know for sure is that my children have eaten more fast food than ever passed my lips as a child.

When my eight-year-old daughter could recite the Dollar Value meals at McDonald's with more accuracy than her times tables, I knew we had a problem.

On my last lap of the day, it was a whole lot easier to speak into a clown's head, drive forward, and have a complete stranger hand me dinner in a paper bag. Whether I was working full-time or as a stay-at-home mom, there wasn't a big difference in our fast-food runs.

Television and magazine human-interest stories scream about American children and their battle with obesity. *I was not helping my children.* Fast food was a poor substitute for a home-cooked meal. Plus, I wasn't raised that way, and I knew better. We were missing out on some great memory-making moments.

When I was a little girl it was our family practice to have dinner together every evening. If my father worked late, Mom waited till Dad got home to serve dinner. We all sat down together as a family, or we didn't eat at all. That's just how it was.

Precious memories were made in that tiny little kitchen in San Lorenzo, California. One evening, when we were very young, my pea-hating sister was ordered by Dad to eat all of the peas on her plate. We knew how much she despised those little green balls of mush. In silence, we watched the first episode of *Fear Factor—Family Edition.* She was the opening act for dinner and a show that night as she washed down each spoonful of peas with a sip of milk.

What she was really doing was spitting her peas into her milk. Not the brightest idea when you are drinking out of a see-through glass. Eventually, the tiny mountain of peas towered above the milk. When Dad figured it out, she got in even bigger trouble and was ordered to drink her milk-peas. I admit it, I laughed until I cried. She just cried.

When my parents purchased our first video camera, the inaugural taping was of the six of us eating dinner together. Figuring out the new tripod, we balanced this huge-by-large camera atop it, carefully placing it in front of our oven to catch every moment of our Friday night pizza dinner.

I belong to a group of hopeless comedians who thought it funny to strategically place large black olives in front of their teeth and talk into the lens. Twenty-five years later, this video is still a hoot at family gatherings. And what a wonderful future blackmail tool in case one of us ever decides to run for public office.

Around our white oval kitchen table there was so much laughter. Sure, there were occasional arguments and tears, but with all of us grown and gone, I'd give anything to eat a meal together around that table again.

8. My minivan was running on fumes.

You can take this one literally or figuratively. I'll leave it to you. Either way, when I was going, going, going, I was more than tired. Is there even a word for "more than tired"? Nope, *exhausted* didn't even come close. Of course, it didn't help that my body was fueled with breakfast on the run and dinner in a bag. If you think we spent a lot of money eating out, you can imagine what we spent filling our gas tank every other day.

7. Something unspeakable was growing in my shower.

Thankfully, my topic is breaking free from the bondage of busyness. If you were expecting to pick up a few housecleaning tips, you'd be disappointed. I have never claimed to be the Alice Brady of the home. *And yes, I know Alice's last name was not Brady.*

Yes, I love a clean house. I just don't enjoy the work involved. I believe with my whole heart that tile grout is a tool to irritate that comes straight from the devil. When you sit at our kitchen table your forearms will more than likely stick to some unseen foreign substance, and I wouldn't be the least bit surprised to discover Amelia Earhart living out her sunset years in one of my closets.

Even with my less-than-stellar housecleaning habits, I still wanted a somewhat orderly home. I didn't have to be able to eat off my bathroom floor, but being able to open the front door without dropping dead from embarrassment was a plus in my book. Stumbling over dirty laundry, scattered toys, or tripping over an open umbrella strategically placed in the middle of our hallway in July was enough to set me off.

When I was in overdrive, the things I should have been doing I wasn't doing at all. And when I wasn't getting my chores done, as you can imagine, my overoccupied children weren't getting *their* chores done either.

6. Be afraid. Be very afraid.

I was irritable *all the time*. My family can vouch for this one. If I am tired, hungry, or hot, they know to tread lightly. I'm not proud of that; I'm just being honest. My darling husband saw the makings of a near perfect storm one summer day a few years ago. While traveling out of town, the temperature soared. There were lots of to-dos on our list that day. It was well above a hundred degrees, and the air conditioner wasn't working. I'd forgotten my purse at our last stop, and traffic was bumper to bumper as we made our way back to retrieve it. I was hungry, tired, and it felt like my body was aflame. Not one of my shining moments.

Busyness became a trigger for explosive outbursts from me. If it isn't grating enough on your nerves to hear your children fighting in the car, listen sometime to what they are fighting about while chauffeuring them from activity to activity. "Don't touch me!" "Stay on your side!" "You stole my pencil!" "I like chocolate way more than you do!" It doesn't take much to set off a busy mom who is already overwhelmed with activity.

5. "Chopsticks" on our back deck equals a romantic night out.

When our children were smaller, this was us. Paul was going to law school during the day and working full-time at night, while I was home caring for the children. Not really your recipe for romance. With four children under the age of nine, we didn't seem to have a moment to brush our teeth, let alone find time together. As much as we enjoyed listening to our daughter play "Chopsticks" on her saxophone, it didn't seem to fill the need for a little romance.

4. Parent guilt: my wallet's worst nightmare.

Parent guilt is well-known among both moms and dads. I experienced this phenomenon most when my children were young and I was working full time. Since I was miserable being away from them all day, I said yes to just about anything they asked for when I was home. When we were out shopping I was even worse. Quantity had replaced quality.

Disney movie? *Sure.*

Barbie dolls? *OK.*

Scooters, roller skates, and large farm animals? *Go ahead, kids, get two.*

I was buying my children, throwing money at a hole in their hearts that could only be filled by time with their mommy. Buying them wasn't working, and their behavior reflected that.

3. Chaos was my closest friend.

My life became a cluttered, confused disarray of disorganization—coupled with a mixed-up, muddled mess of topsy-turvy.

Chaos had become my closest companion. Gone was our sanctuary of peace for my family. When you live like this, it's hard to convince your husband his home really is his castle. What is his incentive to spend time at home when his office at work is more calming? It was difficult to have a relaxed conversation with him about his day, and it was almost impossible for our children to study and get their homework done in the chaos that was our home. Our family life suffered. The kids' schoolwork suffered.

When I was running from place to place, I often wondered what I was running from. *Was I purposely staying away from my home?* The one place that should be our sanctuary from the storms of this world became, instead, one more stressor added to my to-do list.

2. Humming "Jesus Take the Wheel" on the way to a Girl Scout meeting counted as Bible study and quiet time.

How many times had I made excuses for not having my time with the Lord? It was heartbreaking when I stopped and thought about it. I made time for everything else, *including American Idol*, before I devoted a moment of my day to the One who had given me every one of those moments.

"Seven days without the Word makes one weak," was becoming a reality in my life. I considered Bible study by country radio station completely acceptable. I used every excuse to put off opening my Bible and feasting on His Word. How many times had I missed out on godly encouragement, a scriptural treasure from the Lord just for me? It would have made my day so much more bearable.

1. I blinked, and my daughter was seventeen.

It is disturbing to walk into your little girl's room and watch her playing with her baby dolls only to step away for a moment and walk back in as she grabs her car keys and rushes past you, out the door and out of sight. "Enjoy every moment, they grow so fast." If I'd had a nickel for every time I heard that one, I would own Bill Gates.

My Leap of Faith Moment

There was a perfect busyness storm brewing in my life weeks before embarking on our sabbatical. What sparked my list of ten was a book I read, *Leap of Faith* by author and speaker Ellie Lofaro. A story in it haunted me.

While at a women's conference, guest speaker Ellie had been introduced to a beautiful young woman who was in the final stages of cancer. Terminally ill, this mommy of two encouraged the women in her family to attend the conference together. Ellie noticed how this sick woman's joy was contagious.

Later, Ellie padded down the hall in her pajamas, still inspired and oddly curious, to find this woman and have a word with her.

When she arrived at the young woman's hotel room, she found what appeared to be a slumber party. It wasn't long before she was a part of the fun. She hated to leave. But before Ellie headed back to her own room, she decided to ask one question. Turning toward the cancer-stricken woman—a young woman staring at her own mortality—she asked, "What is it I can share with future women? What words of wisdom can I share from you?"

Without missing a beat, the woman answered, "Don't pin your hopes on living."

That hit me like a bucket of ice water dumped on my head; I was chilled to the bone. *Don't pin your hopes on living.* For days that statement kept coming back to me. Still, as I write this, I am surprised by the power it has over me.

I was thirty years old when I was shaken for the first time by the reality of my own mortality. Sitting in an emergency room has a way of doing that to you. My mother had been rushed to the hospital by ambulance and was subsequently diagnosed with a brain tumor. At the much-too-young age of fifty-two, I couldn't believe stage four cancer was possible. Mothers weren't supposed to die. Certainly not in their fifties. Not in their forties. Not ever. I'd taken for granted she would be there for my lifetime of joys and heartaches. I never once thought she wouldn't be around to watch me raise my babies into adulthood. It was clear now; I had made a huge mistake. I'd pinned my hopes on her living.

The reality of my own mortality hit me. How important was my busyness? As I came to terms with my denial, my list, the book, and a conversation with a girlfriend were my call to arms to stop living for when my babies no longer took naps, when they were potty-trained, when they started school, when they grew up, next week, next month, next year, when we have money, when we have the time. Except, *I did have time.*

God was orchestrating circumstances to prepare my heart to make a radical decision. I was tired of running. I was ready for change.

Dear Lord, thank you for dropping bread crumbs of ideas and encouragement in the books I read, the friends I speak with, and even the lists I write. Thank you for being the soft whisper in the circumstances of my life. Help me see where I can cut away burdensome things. Help me to pin my hope on you. In Jesus' name I pray. Amen.

- Make your own top ten list of things you want to do with your family this year.
- Have you ever known someone whose time on earth seemed too short? What do you think he or she would tell you about your list?
- Are you a runner? Hang up your running shoes this weekend. Invite your children to hang up theirs too.

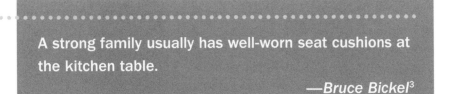

A strong family usually has well-worn seat cushions at the kitchen table.

—*Bruce Bickel*[3]

PART II

Breakthrough

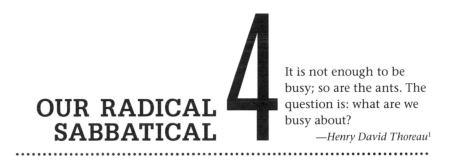

OUR RADICAL SABBATICAL

4

It is not enough to be busy; so are the ants. The question is: what are we busy about?

—Henry David Thoreau[1]

All around the mulberry bush the monkey chased the weasel. The monkey thought it was all in fun. POP goes the weasel! That was me. Just like that silly little weasel being continually pursued by an irritating monkey, I was running every day, round and round that mulberry bush, and I was about to *POP*. There is more truth to that well-loved nursery rhyme than parents care to admit. Round and round life goes—our days and weeks becoming busier and busier—until eventually, something has to give.

I was just about at my popping point when friends invited our family over for a New Year's Eve celebration. Our children and theirs were all about the same ages and got along really well. As soon as we arrived, the kids piled out of the car and ran off in different directions, and the husbands retreated to the family room to watch a basketball game. This gave my friend and me a chance for some much-needed girl time.

Our conversation quickly moved to our children and the busyness of our lives. Soon we began to play one of our favorite mom games, busy-mom poker. The topic of this poker game was what else? Busyness.

I'll see your basketball practices on Monday, Tuesday, and Wednesday nights and raise you a 6:30 A.M. school bus drop-off time, three dozen homemade cupcakes for the bake sale on Friday, and a soccer game this weekend in Antarctica.

My friend shared the demands basketball and Girl Scouts brought to their lives, while I shared with her how thrilled I was we finally had a breather in December after our soccer season ended in November. Kim went on to share how she was already dreading summer. Three of her four children swam on a local swim team. This meant she would spend at least two of their three summer months at the swimming pool dragging all of her four children to sit for hours each day. Now, add some very hot triple-digit summer days and thousands of minutes playing red light/green light with her youngest child, and you have the recipe for a nuclear bomb—or a mother who might go nuclear.

We were friends sitting together, commiserating over our bondage of busyness and our captivity of activity. After commiserating for a while, I shared the story with her I'd read and the haunting words still with me: *Don't pin your hopes on living.*[2]

"This dying mother had less than six months to live," I shared.

"How sad," Kim said.

That mother understood how precious every moment is, I thought. I shared with my girlfriend how I wanted to live like that—with purpose. I wanted to make my time count. Life is too short to be wasting even a moment of it.

When I stopped to think about it, how important, in the grand scheme of things, were all of these activities we were involved in?

**My friend said softly, almost to herself,
"I wish we could take a whole year off and not do a thing."**

The moment those words left her lips, I had my epiphany. "Why can't we?" Like a mad scientist, the thought seemed absurd, even to me. Yet my heart was almost giddy with joy. My friend chuckled, and her laugh surprised me. I really meant what I said. Leaning forward in my chair I stared directly into her eyes, "Why can't we take a year off from all outside activities? Tell our kids *no* for one year. Can you imagine how great it would be to take a break?" I could tell she liked the idea too.

In seconds, her facial expression changed, "Chris would never let me do it. He wants the kids to be on the swim team. I've tried, Joanne. He wants them all to swim."

"Well, my friend, you never know until you ask," I said, sounding more confident then I felt. Right on cue our husbands came strolling in. They had no idea the ambush awaiting them. Looking up at her husband, Kim went first. "Chris, what do you think about taking a break? Taking a year off from all outside activities, even swim team?"

Looking at her as if she'd just asked to paint his toenails a lovely shade of pink, Chris laughed. Before she could protest, he went on to give every good reason their kids needed to be on the swim team.

Kim just looked at me and smirked, as if to say, *I told you so.* Now it was my turn, sitting back in my chair, legs tucked under me, I looked up at my husband and prepared to state my case.

"Paul, Kim and I have been talking about the insanity of driving our kids back and forth every day like a taxi driver and came up with a great idea. What do you think about taking a year off? Taking a break? No after-school activities for the kids this year." My turn now over, I silently waited for him to answer. Never hesitating, Paul smiled, "I think it sounds like a great idea."

Knowing my husband as well as I do, I had a feeling he would be all for it. He is always up for a challenge. Now it was my turn to make a commitment, to shake hands on the deal. Frankly, I wanted to back out; I was scared. *No activities for the children for a year? What was I thinking?* My son loved playing soccer. My daughter looked forward to her weekly voice lessons. Saying it was one thing, but doing it was a whole other story.

While I was thinking, Kim watched me. I knew she was waiting to see whether or not I would follow through. My mouth went dry, but my pride won out. "OK, then that's what we're going to do." My words came out with more conviction than I felt. The gauntlet had been thrown.

Driving home, I couldn't believe what I agreed to do, and in front of witnesses no less. *What would our year be like without organized activities? How were we going to tell the children? What would they say? Me and my big mouth! Would I even be able to stick to this? Well, it wasn't the first time my big mouth had written a check reality couldn't cash.* My husband and I went to bed praying about this whole idea.

And I fell asleep silently praying he would forget all about it.

The next morning we had a delicious New Year's Day breakfast planned. My husband and I prayed together in our bedroom before greeting our four children. They ran to us, all crying "Happy New Year!" They were in great moods for having little sleep the night before, which didn't help my nerves one bit. We were about to crush their little hearts. They had no idea what was coming.

Our family tradition every New Year's Day is to have a big breakfast followed by devotions together. I don't remember exactly what scripture in the Bible my husband shared with us, but I do know we shared thankfulness for the past year and spoke of our goals and what we desired for our year ahead. It was during this family time we explained in detail our new plan with the children.

Everyone, stuffed from breakfast and still in their pajamas, had migrated to their lounging positions around the family room when I broke the news.

"We are going to do something as a family this year, something quite different, and something no family has ever done—that we know of. We are going to take an activity time out."

You could have heard crickets; not one child said a word. Our youngest two were only five and seven and didn't have the faintest idea what I was talking about. Our oldest two were twelve and fifteen and knew exactly what we were saying. They were in shock.

Their father continued where I left off. "For the next twelve months there will be no soccer, no baseball, no voice lessons, and no community theater. Anything you want to do that requires your mom to drive you there will be considered an activity and will receive a resounding *no* from the both of us."

They all clearly understood our plan now, and joy left the room. I was waiting for shrieks and tears and fits of anger. What we received instead were some deer-in-the-headlights looks from our teenagers and a few *Aaawwww mans* from the younger children, who had finally figured it out and understood some of our new plan. I was amazed. Where were the shrieks and tears? Maybe they didn't think we were going to actually do this.

Before we'd met the kids at breakfast, Paul and I had time to discuss an idea I'd come up with. Now it was time I shared it with the children. "Each month this year we are going to have a monthly family field trip."

Their dad took a breath and continued, "One Saturday each month will be set apart for family fun. Each of you will get a chance to pick one of our monthly adventures this year."

The kids, still rendered almost speechless, hadn't said much. But at least they were listening to us. Very thankful there wasn't any big mutiny, I threw my Hail Mary pass and appealed to their hearts. "We love all of you so very much, but being so busy is not giving us any quality time together. We are passing each other like ships in the night." Moving my head back and forth from one pair of beautiful eyes to the next, I fought to hold back tears. "Your father and I only have so many years at home with all of you, only so much time together before you are grown and gone with your own little ones. As much as we love watching you play soccer games and baseball games, let's start taking advantage of this God-given time we have together."

Thankfully, they seemed to accept that, or they could have been afraid I was going to start blubbering. Paul pulled out our brand-spankin'-new wall calendar. We sat down with the kids and penciled in one Saturday each month we were going to set aside for a family field trip. The children soon gathered around, voicing their ideas for their chosen months, chattering like parakeets. Within a matter of moments, joy once again flooded the room.

Well, the hard part was over; we had told the kids. When we went to church the next week I excitedly shared with our pastor our New Year's resolution. I told him we'd decided to take a break from activities and put a kibosh on our busyness. "What a great idea." He smiled and said, "You're taking a *radical sabbatical.*"

"Yes," I said, smiling back. "That's exactly what we're doing." I just loved that, *a radical sabbatical.* Our pastor knew our family was definitely not afraid of being guinea pigs for the congregation.

Our parents were also excited about the possibility of seeing us more than just Christmas or on the sidelines at a soccer field. I couldn't begin to count the times we had told them we couldn't meet them, couldn't stop by, and couldn't call them right back because we were too busy. Now they had hope in seeing us more. They had said to us so many times, "These days go by quickly. Before you know it, your children will be all grown up. Enjoy every moment together." In their eyes, we had made a commitment to do just that.

Like salmon running upstream, we committed to go against everything we knew and everything that seemed to make any sense at all for a whole year. When we began our radical sabbatical in January, we were rejecting the captivity of activity. We didn't know it then, but what we were really saying was *yes* to a year of memories and quite a few life lessons that none of us will soon forget.

Dear Lord, I praise you for this idea. You use the foolish things of the world to confound the wise, and, Lord, you know just how foolish this radical sabbatical sounded to me when I first picked up this book. I would love so much to have a year off without self-induced obligations. Help me, Lord, to be of one mind with my husband and take our very own radical sabbatical. In Jesus' name I pray. Amen.

- What activity is causing you the greatest burden? How can you scale back your time commitment?
- Are you making a point to spend time together as a family? When was the last time you did?
- Let your children mark a date on the calendar each month to spend a morning, afternoon, or evening together. If you're a family of overachievers, plan to spend the whole day together!

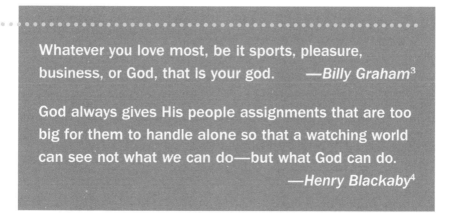

Whatever you love most, be it sports, pleasure, business, or God, that is your god.   —*Billy Graham*[3]

God always gives His people assignments that are too big for them to handle alone so that a watching world can see not what *we* can do—but what God can do.
—*Henry Blackaby*[4]

TWELVE MONTHS OF FIELD TRIPS

The best inheritance a parent can give his children is a few minutes of his time each day.

—*O. A. Battista*[1]

I hate field trips. There aren't words to describe my deep disdain for all things field trip. The moment the permission slip makes it home and finds its way out of my child's backpack and into my hands, I silently scream, *Oh, no! Not another trip to the zoo!*

I've been to planetariums, science museums, community farms, and in our case, Coloma. For those of you not up on your California history, Coloma is the spot on the map where, thanks to John Marshall, gold was discovered. This year marked my third field trip to the quaint little gold-rush town.

I know this field trip so well I can finish the tour guide's sentences. "Keep your hands to yourselves. Be respectful. No food, gum, or drinks inside the museum. And make sure to use your inside voices."

What are inside voices anyway? It's the voice I use every time my son or daughter shoves a note from their teacher under my nose requesting my presence on a miserable ride with a busload of children—many of whom don't obey, *ever*. And surprise, surprise, wouldn't you know it? One of those kids is always in my group. Coloma field trip number three was no exception.

Even with my mutant field trip gene, I was still able to plaster a smile on my face when my little girl panned for gold and made a leather satchel to hold her priceless discoveries. I even kind of enjoyed hiking up the side of the mountain with my daughter to see where John Marshall was buried—have I mentioned *for the third time?*

I wasn't surprised when I landed my next "acting gig" a year later. The Lord knows my field trip weakness, and I believe He wants me to grow in this area.

If there were an academy award for Actress in a Leading Role as a Mother who Loves Field Trips, I'd be a shoo-in.

My most recent field trip memory plays over and over in my head, taken from my own private field trip posttraumatic stress disorder file.

"Mom, you've been chosen!" My daughter looked like she'd run all the way home from school. Perspiration collected on her top lip.

"For what?" I asked, turning away from the kitchen sink.

"You've been picked!" she squealed. "Only a handful of parents are picked, and you've been chosen!"

"Picked for what, Grace?" Her excitement was contagious and I started jumping up and down with her.

"For our coast trip, Mom! Don't you remember? I gave you that paper, and you checked the box by your name that said yes!"

When had I marked "yes" on a form? I tried to think quickly.

In a flash, it came to me. *Oh, no, not the fifth grade coast trip.*

The room began to spin. I stopped jumping. How could this be? I'd hedged my bet when I'd shown interest. I'd worked the numbers. The odds were against me. There were more than enough crazy parents who loved sleeping in the forest and lying on dirt for days at a time. My name was picked? *O Lord, what went wrong?*

Grace was watching me now. Instantly, I threw myself back into character—Spielberg would have been impressed.

"Oh, *that* piece of paper. Now I remember. Of course! How wonderful, Honey. I'm so excited we get to go together." Running up to me, she threw her arms around my waist and we jumped up and down once again.

It was true. My name had been one of a handful chosen to chaperone a five-day camping trip with seventy-three fifth graders. Have I mentioned I don't camp?

- Day One: I landed the 11 P.M. to 1 A.M. watch for wild animals. Foxes and raccoons are more frightening than you think.
- Day Two: It rained—hard. Parents, drenched like ship rats, ran around the campground digging trenches around tents. Others warmed wet, whimpering children under hair dryers in the public restroom where the showers had quit working on Day One.
- Day Three: I smiled through soggy sandwiches. As my stomach rumbled, my mind flashed back to a few weeks earlier. "Mom! Look what I have." Grace ran in waving a sheet of paper above her head. "It's the list of our meals for the trip next week. Our group got to pick each meal ourselves. We are going to have hot dogs, Top Ramen, Funions . . ."

  "Wow. Hot dogs *and* Funions *and* Top Ramen. Yuuummmyyy!" I smiled. Holding back my gag reflex and pretending to lick my lips as I hugged her.
- Day Four: I couldn't help but think of all of the veteran parents who had gone before me. Certainly I was not alone. I couldn't possibly be the only parent allergic to bus rides to strange places with screaming fifth graders.
- Day Five: I don't recall. I've blocked it.

God takes field trips to a whole new level.

Hours before we shared our radical sabbatical idea with the children, no one was more surprised than me when I blurted, "Paul, why don't we let the children pick a family fun day each month? It could be a monthly adventure." Translation: a family field trip. Yes, I love hanging out with my family. I really do. But I saw the flashing red lights—sealing my family-day fate on our calendar. It screamed, "Field trip!" to me.

I quickly pushed the voices aside and forged ahead. Like every diet, I start off strong. I am a true blue zealot. This was the same attitude that reared its ugly head when we took the children on their first family field trip adventure.

January

We brought a picnic lunch to a local park and stopped on the way to the ice rink. After paying quite a bit of money to fall down on hard ice many times, we took the children to a movie matinee. Afterward, we ate at McDonald's for dinner. The whole day ended up costing us almost $100.

Later that night, after doing the math, my husband and I were not pleased. It was clear our wallets paid for the guilt we carried about not letting our children participate in their regular activities. I think we subconsciously tried to buy them and ease our radical sabbatical remorse. January was an over-the-top family field trip. Not only was it expensive, but it was extremely busy. We were slow learners.

February

In February, the choices for our family day were much different. On the first Saturday in February, the city of Sacramento has a free admission day for the community. We had a long list of museums, a zoo, and community parks to visit that day. We decided to let each child pick a museum of his or her liking.

Our first destination was the zoo. Later, we stopped by the military museum, the aerospace museum, and then we were off to the historical cemetery. We actually brought our bag lunches there and ate them as the cemetery docent gave us a tour of all the aged crypts and plots. We walked along as she shared fascinating stories about the people buried there.

At the end of the day, we realized that if we had paid admissions it would have cost us more than $300. We were getting better at finding fun things to do that wouldn't break our piggy bank, but we were still caught up in the busyness of the day. *Will we ever break free from the captivity of activity?* I wondered.

March

March was a breakthrough month for me. It was my turn to pick the family day, and my choice was a trip to Daffodil Hill. The children groaned when I penciled it in on the calendar. Forty-five minutes from our home, tucked away in the foothills, is the most precious little farm. It's open to the public for only a few weeks each spring—just enough time to witness 300,000 daffodils open for their annual moment of glory.

There really isn't much to do there—a small petting zoo, a picnic area, and a small playground. When I remembered how little there was for the kids, I almost caved and erased my choice from the calendar. A flashback from when I was a teenager stopped me.

We didn't have a lot of money growing up, which meant we rarely took family vacations. When my siblings and I caught wind that our parents had a getaway in the works, we couldn't wait to hear where they planned to take us. Visions of Disneyland danced in our heads. When we discovered we would be driving our nine-passenger, wood-paneled station wagon to the Redwood Forest in Northern California, we were devastated. Twenty-five years later, my siblings and I still joke about stopping at a fish hatchery and taking a tour of a lumber mill, none of which were at the top of a child's dream vacation destinations.

My mom and dad's second attempt at taking us on a family vacation looked to be a winner. We would be staying at a cabin in Lake Tahoe. My siblings and I were ecstatic. On top of our vehicle, my dad tied down an inner tube for our fun in the lake. You need to understand something here. This wasn't your ordinary inner tube. My aunt worked for an airline, which meant she was able to get her hands on an inner tube from a real airplane tire. Have you ever seen the size of an airplane tire?

There is nothing more traumatizing to a seventeen-year-old girl then having an inflated inner tube only the Jolly Green Giant could appreciate strapped to the top of a nine-passenger, wood-paneled station wagon.

Actually, there is one thing more traumatizing: hearing your father yell "Oh, no!" moments before your arrival. I sat rigid and mortified, staring straight ahead, willing myself invisible, like any good teenager, as an audience of cars witnessed an obscenely elephantine inner tube bounce off our station wagon, down the freeway, and out of sight.

After putting the begrudged family field trip into perspective, I no longer feared our children's disappointed pleas. As is His nature, God didn't disappoint. On the day we embarked on our children's unfavorite destination to Daffodil Hill, we stopped alongside a remote area to have a picnic.

As we sat and ate our mountaintop picnic lunch, thousands of butterflies fluttered by. We found ourselves smack dab in the middle of their migration route. We didn't even know butterflies migrated.

Our random stop was God's intended blessing.

The children laughed and skipped around, pointing and shouting for us to look at each splendid specimen that fluttered by. While we ate peanut butter and jelly sandwiches, around us danced breathtakingly colorful mountaintop fairies. It was magical.

April

In April we spent three days hunkered down together with snow and crock pot chili, courtesy of our dear family friends who own a cabin in Lake Tahoe and are gracious enough to let us use it each year. We made memories sledding, reading, eating lots of peanut M&M's, and watching *The Lord of the Rings* trilogy.

May

When the kids chirped from the backseat, asking if we were lost, Paul responded, "No, of course not. You can't be lost with a full tank of gas."

We may not have known where we were headed, but God knew. In the morning we began our adventure by loading up the cooler and heading in a direction we'd never been before. Eating our lunch in an area of tall rocks, the kids played and climbed to their hearts' content. We stumbled upon a beautiful lake high in the mountains. The kids were a bit stir-crazy after a two-hour drive and piled out of our Suburban in record time.

Nothing says mom-joy like watching your children work together to canoe around a lake. My sweet prayer of thankfulness was interrupted by a very loud argument. Apparently, Samuel, our youngest, refused to wear his life vest. This infuriated his big sister, Grace, who works undercover as his second mother. As Grace screamed and yelled at Samuel, Meghan and David decided to have a water fight with their oars with Grace caught in the crossfire.

I learned three things from the May field trip.

- Sound carries on water.
- Grace has a future with the Metropolitan Opera.
- Not every monthly outing was going to be picture perfect.

June

By June we realized a field trip didn't have to be an all-day thing. We were slowly learning quality not quantity was king. When we discovered our children had never been to a drive-in movie, June's field trip was born. We gave each child a dollar and let him or her choose candy at a nearby Dollar Store before embarking on our next adventure.

We'd learned that our local drive-in movie had a Tuesday discount night. Tuesday became our new Saturday for the month of June. The kids didn't mind a bit.

Paul backed up his pickup and parked in a perfect spot. Our four were immediately arranging sleeping bags and pillows to watch the movie under the stars in the truck bed. They were thrilled.

July

When dad made his choice for our July family fun day, no one was surprised. Being the boring—*ahem*—I mean patient and steadfast man he is, he chose a day at home to do nothing. Did I say nothing? I mean absolutely nothing. We hung out all day, eating, reading, talking, listening to music, and ended the day with a family movie. It was perfect.

August

The blackberry farms in our area are ripe for the picking in August, so we chose this month to pick lots of them. It didn't take long before all six of us were armed with tin buckets and ready for our mission to find the biggest and sweetest. As a family, we can be a bit competitive, so pails filled quickly.

On a warm summer day, with blue-stained fingers, we ate our picnic lunch under the shade of an oak tree while the kids played with a Frisbee. Our monthly time together was beginning to slow down immensely.

September

In Camino, California, there is a small area of farms known as Apple Hill. Each fall, people drive from all over to enjoy fresh produce, home-baked sugary treats, and a simpler time. We spent our September family field trip at Apple Hill.

Apple Hill is not foreign to us. We are some of their biggest fans. We have our favorite farms and must-haves when we ride up for the day. Paul loves the "walking pie," a large softball-sized piece of warm apple pie enclosed in crust. I enjoy the blueberry sour cream pie, while the kids are always up for a caramel apple or a scoop of apple ice cream. We made sure to bring our picnic lunch and sit in a shaded spot before going from farm to farm. The day was a success.

October ▪ November ▪ December

As the weeks passed, our monthly family field trips became more and more relaxed. We were surprised to experience what an actual weekend felt like with no obligations. What a foreign concept!

With our family experiment quickly coming to a close, our oldest daughter, Meghan, decided how we would spend our special day together in October. Being fifteen years old, I expected she would choose an expensive outing with lots of activity. I silently wondered how soon I would have to tell her no because of the expense of what she wanted us to do.

After giving her a few suggestions, I waited for her to speak.

"Mom, can we just stay at home and hang out all day in our pajamas?" Her words stopped me cold.

I couldn't believe what I was hearing! After almost a year, we were finally learning how to stop, how to say *no* to the good things, and how to say *yes* to the best thing of all—time together as a family. Meghan's choice for October was so well-received we chose the very same family time for November and December too.

Like salmon running upstream, for a whole year we went against everything we knew and everything that seemed to make any sense at all. We began our radical sabbatical in January by saying *no* to the captivity of activity and *yes* to a year of family memories that weren't seen in a blur but were carefully filed away for the future.

Dear Lord, help me stop for the special moments we sometimes rush past. Remind me that we don't need lots of money to have a picnic at a park or read a book together under a shady tree. Give me the strength to do things even when the children protest, and give me patience to see the blessing in the not-so-perfect family field trip. In Jesus' name I pray. Amen.

- Gather your children and seek their input for a future family field trip together.
- Surprise your family by loading them up and taking them somewhere they've never been before. Make sure to take along some books and a ball.
- Get a map of your local parks. Visit one a week until you've seen them all together.

TWO OUT OF THREE AIN'T BAD

Ask a child what he wants for dinner only if he's buying.

—*Fran Lebowitz*[1]

"How in the world did you get your kids to go along with this radical sabbatical?" I'm a little surprised every time I get this question, because for the most part, the parent asking me this question usually seems almost afraid to consider such a thing. Yet they want to hear more. They seem almost unable to allow themselves an inkling of the potential joy of even thinking of ways they can curb their busy schedules. Because, my goodness, what would the kids do without—whatever?

Our children are not perfect and neither are their parents. Though, my husband would disagree. Our sabbatical didn't begin with a loud bang or any fanfare at all really. I had earned a bad reputation for saying things and not having a very powerful follow through, which worked in my favor for once, because they immediately thought I wouldn't have the fortitude to follow through with this wacky new idea. Once the kids realized I was serious, and their father was even more serious, they weren't thrilled at beginning this family adventure.

I asked my oldest daughter, our family's most faithful diary keeper, to look over her sabbatical year diary and see if she'd written anything specifically about her frustrations with her parents and our radical activity change. Surprisingly, the anger and frustration penned about us her sophomore year in high school was about curfews and girlfriends. The only words that made it into her journals from our sabbatical were positive affirmations from our family excursions. I consider that a very good thing.

I'm not a sociopath who desires to watch my children writhe in pain. My husband and I knew this break was best for all of us, and whether they chose to write or remember the sabbatical in a positive or negative light, we weren't going to be deterred.

There wasn't a door slammed or a disrespectful word exclaimed in my presence about our sabbatical. If they happened, it was funneled through disappointment or anger over other things. Our kids were smart enough to shout them into their pillow or share them quietly with one another. David was the child who shared his thoughts more than the rest, and I've documented the few I recall. So, I thought it might be helpful to let you meet our children. With Meghan, now an adult and away at college, I've saved her personal thoughts and words for the next chapter. My prayer is for you to see a bit of your own child in one of ours.

Little League Pitcher Sits the Bench

David is our second child and oldest son. Born on a sweltering hot day in August, he was a tiny bundle of slick brown hair, baby acne, and red blotchy complexion. When I brought him home from the hospital I thought he resembled a middle-aged golfer with a drinking problem.

I held David in my arms and wondered, *How in the world do I raise a little boy?* I soon discovered the gender of my second child mattered very little. I loved David and David loved me. It was the beginning of a beautiful relationship.

I'd been told by mothers with boys how special it was to have a son. I quickly learned they were right. David was full of kisses and cuddles and was a little boy through and through. We learned very early on never to bend down and cup our hands if he ran into the house yelling, "Mommy, Daddy, I have something for you!"

At four years old, this child could scoop up field mice with his bare hands and catch chicken hawks out of midair. He loved his yellow lab, Tylo, like a twin sister, and when she died, he slept with her collar for weeks. The hiccupping sobs of an eleven-year-old boy, pleading with God to bring his best friend back for just one more minute, seared my mother's heart for all my days. Unbeknownst to him, on the other side of his bedroom wall I sobbed into my own pillow, praying to the very same God, asking Him to take away my son's hurt.

David would tell you today he would never do a sabbatical with his kids. He was the most hostile toward our sabbatical year. Our son is a gifted athlete, and what he lacked in desire to complete junior high homework he more than made up for in sports. He was pitching for his little league baseball team the year before we took our family break. David wasn't one to have tantrums, but he made sure those twelve months were made memorable by as much verbal judo as possible. I found it interesting when he recently told me he was going on an iPod fast.

"What did you just say?" I asked him, trying not to drop my salad tongs and make the moment as big as I believed it was.

"I'm not going to use my iPod all day tomorrow. I've been using it too much lately. I want to experience a whole day without it." He said it like it was no big deal and walked out of the kitchen, leaving me with my mouth hanging wide open.

As a parent, we understand our big moments sometimes come wrapped up in little moments. So I was relishing this one. How many almost sixteen-year-olds would realize they were spending too much time with anything and walk away from whatever it was because they thought it was occupying too much of their lives?

David could protest all he wanted about his kooky sabbatical family and his rebel mom who liked to do things differently. He was beginning to live the very same way.

When the Lord opened the door for our radical sabbatical, we dragged David through it with us. As a teenager, David enjoys the peace and quiet of our home, and although he is the extroverted type A life-of-the-party, he will retreat to his room "to think" if things get too chaotic at our house.

An added bonus to our sabbatical year is that we inadvertently showed our son that walking through God's open door always yields a blessing on the other side. He took this to heart a few years later.

God Opens the Door to the Land Down Under

When God opened the door for David to work on our friend's three thousand acre sheep ranch in Australia, Paul and I encouraged him to walk through it. My husband saw a great opportunity for a lesson on hard work. "No, Son, we won't help you buy your $200 passport or your $1,000 ticket. You and the Lord will have to work that out together."

His friends thought he was nuts when he shared he was raising money for a trip Down Under. "Your parents won't even let you have a cell phone, but they'll let you go on a plane halfway across the world, *alone?*"

David proceeded to earn enough money refereeing soccer games and babysitting every child within a five-mile radius to purchase his passport and a pig for the Future Farmers of America program at his high school. He raised his first pig to third place in our local county fair and auctioned it off to earn his ticket to Australia.

To David's friends, his trip to Australia seemed a bit radical. At almost sixteen years of age, our son's plane landed on Australian soil before his forty-something parents had passports of their own.

I believe our radical sabbatical way of living played a part in his once-in-a-lifetime trip.

Goosey Gander Hangs Up Her Cleats

Ruth Bell Graham once said of her daughter Bunny, "She was born good."[2] The same is true about our daughter Grace.

Sitting in the number three slot in the pecking order, she might very well be the sweetest child the Lord ever created.

Our daughter Grace is nicknamed Goose, or Goosey Gander. She wasn't very happy to miss soccer for a year when she was eight years old. She once said, "I want the boys in my class to know I've got game."

If anyone asks about our children, Paul and I like to explain them this way: "We have two head-kids and two heart-kids." Meghan and Samuel, our oldest and youngest, would be our head kids. They are thinkers. If we talk with them or ask them something, they use their heads first. For them, logic immediately takes over before a clear and precise decision can be rendered. David and Grace, the two sandwiched in the middle of our four, are our heart-kids. These two think with their hearts first. Whatever decisions need to be made are sifted through feelings and emotions.

Being a heart-kid doesn't mean you've been hit a few times with a dumb-stick. On the contrary, Grace is in the gifted program at school and an A student. Being a heart-kid just means there are lots more of those "Awwwwww, how sweet" moments when she's involved.

There are tender memories stored up in my mind's library of Grace wearing her heart on her little-girl sleeve.

While in Disneyland, we'd just placed Grace, four years old at the time, and Samuel, age two, in a spot in the audience where they could watch the live *Toy Story* show in action. The rest of us sat in chairs about fifty feet away. When Buzz Lightyear's archenemy Zerg came onstage, *key the loud, scary music*, Grace panicked. Trying to rescue her brother from potential disaster, we watched as she was the only child out of hundreds who pulled and tugged on her little brother's arm, frantically trying to drag him away from impending doom. Her brother struggled to stay right where he was. Amid a sea of toddlers, Grace worked to pull her not-very-happy baby brother to safety.

Grace was the only child who had a "moment" in regard to our radical sabbatical. You see, the euphoria of making a good change came to a screeching halt only days after announcing our sabbatical to the kids. We were at Baskin Robbins, enjoying dollar-a-scoop night, when Grace's former soccer coach walked in.

Teachers, coaches, and pastors all have celebrity status when seen in public by children. And our children are no exception to that rule. Grace was so excited. Knowing her coach enjoyed ice cream like she did put him at the top of the celebrity A-list in her eyes.

Walking over to our table, he asked our little girl, "So, Grace, are you going to play on my team again this year?"

Smiling, she nodded her head furiously up and down. "Yes!" She smiled.

"Good! Then I'll see you in a couple of months," he said over his shoulder as he walked out of the store.

Paul and I just looked at each other. Figured. This whole radical sabbatical thing had been way too easy so far. My heart about broke when I gently reminded Grace we were taking a break this year, and that included her and her soccer team too. She looked at me with such puppy dog eyes. I felt miserable. We hid our sad hearts, and I encouraged her, "Honey, even without soccer, this year is going to be one that you'll never forget. I promise." I reminded her, "God has a great year ahead of us. Just wait and see." I wasn't sure if those words of encouragement were for her or for me.

Since our little Grace was down in the dumps and it was her birthday month—January, we were happy that it was her pick for the first family field trip of the year. Grace is the reason Paul and I ended up on ice skates for the first time in twenty years. I've often wondered if this was her passive-aggressive way of punishing us. Maybe she isn't as sweet as we think.

Our Little Caboose Parks It in the Station

**If I believed in aliens, I'd be convinced
I was a nine-month pod for our youngest son.**

Samuel looks almost nothing like me, with the exception of my light hair and deep green eyes; he's his father's clone. He looks like a four-foot nine replica of my Paul. He has the same analytical mind and even received the coveted puts-things-back gene. I think it's a mutation, but my husband insists it's genetic.

Samuel is happiest with a video controller in his hands and finds joy in reading his favorite author, Bryan Davis, and riding his bike with his big brother to our neighborhood Caffé Santoro to buy an ice cream cone. He's the youngest of our four and brings up the rear. He is my baby. But please don't tell him I said that. He tries with all his might to do everything his brother does. Anyone who knows our family knows Samuel adores David.

Now nine, he was only six years old when we took our sabbatical. Samuel remembers almost nothing, which should come as some comfort for any of you reading this with younger children yourself. I'm not even sure the memories he spouts are from his own memory bank or borrowed from the continually changing war stories shared by his older siblings.

He had already played one season of soccer by the time we took a break. So he did know a little bit about what he was missing that year. I loved watching his team play. They all looked so tiny running on the field; their shorts almost looked like long pants as they swarmed like honeybees trying to kick at the ball.

Samuel still remembers his friend asking him in his kindergarten class, "Why aren't you going to play soccer this year, Sam?" Samuel tried to convince me it scarred him for life when I asked him about it today at lunch. As this never-before-heard story went on and on, my eyes narrowed, and he had a hard time keeping a straight face through his mouthful of peanut butter sandwich.

What Do You Think?

In order to help you see three of my children's perspectives on our radical sabbatical, I asked them to answer a few questions for me. I wanted you to know what they thought about our year-long break.

What do you remember about our radical sabbatical?

David: That it was very uneventful.

Grace: Having Dad show me how to ice skate.

Samuel: All the horrid time without sports!

What was the toughest part about taking a radical sabbatical?

David: I think it ruined my baseball skills.

Grace: Not being able to play soccer.

Samuel: Doing no sports.

Would you recommend a radical sabbatical to your friends or take one with your own family when you're a parent?

David: No, it was dumb and had no point.

Grace: Yes, because I think it's important to spend time with your family so you will have great memories for a lifetime.

Samuel: Yes and yes, because it is good family bonding time.

David is in the middle of his teenage years, so I believe him completely when he shares how the sabbatical was dumb and had no point. I'm sure that's how he feels, for now. Thankfully, I know something he doesn't know: he still has a bit of maturing to do. That's the very reason I asked our oldest, Meghan, to share in her own words about her radical experience in the next chapter. Since she's the only one of our four with an adult perspective, I think you'll find it very interesting. As far as my youngest three children are concerned, well, two out of three ain't bad.

Dear Lord, you created me with the ability to raise my children. Fill me with the strength to be the parent they need and not just the one they want. Remind me when things don't always go the way they had hoped that sometimes those are the ways you had hoped. Fill me with your Holy Spirit so I can walk each day in your strength, especially days I'm not voted the most popular by my kids. In Jesus' name I pray. Amen.

- Do your children see you as a follow-through parent or a parent who lacks perseverance?
- Do you consider a parenting decision successful only if everyone is happy?
- Beware of wanting your children to be happy all the time.
- Ask your children to share their favorite family memory.

REFLECTIONS OF A SABBATICAL SURVIVOR

Every day with teenagers
is like the final two days
of a five-year pregnancy.
—*Erma Bombeck*[1]

Meghan is the oldest of our four children. She's our official guinea pig. I was twenty-three years old when she was born. As she grew in size, I tried to grow alongside her in motherly wisdom. Through year fifteen to sixteen, she experienced being part of a family in which doing things a little radically soon became the norm.

As the oldest, she's the natural leader of our children, although her siblings would probably define her as *bossy*. As a little girl, she loved to play make-believe. She could spend hours encouraging her Barbie dolls to act out her grammar school dreams on a maroon carpet stage. Barbie dolls were eventually replaced by her first true love—books. Her junior high girlfriends thought it was funny—and a bit odd—when we put her on a week's restriction from reading. Her nose was forever stuffed between the bindings of a book.

Meghan was student of the year at her grammar school, gave the junior high graduation speech, and enrolled in every accelerated class available in high school, lettering in academics. Who would have known the dimpled blonde cherub who stole my heart the moment she was born would grow up to be so goal-oriented? Meghan was quite possibly our has-it-all-together kid. Her poor attitude seemed to balance the scales.

You can tread water longer than they can make it rain.

I can still remember the day our daughter began junior high. Everything changed. In a matter of minutes we went from being the greatest parents in the world to the worst—at least according to her. Parents formerly known as smart, funny, and friendly became ignorant, out-of-touch, and embarrassing overnight.

Just as she had done at the age of two, our daughter questioned *every single solitary thing.* I've come to realize just how much teenagers and two-year-olds have in common.

Why? *Because we said so.* How come? *Because we love you.* Why are you and Dad so strict? *We're sorry you feel that way.* Why don't you trust me? *It's not you we don't trust.* Emily is going, why can't I? *We'd tell Emily no, too, if we were her parents.* You don't want me to have fun. *How'd you guess?* You don't care about me. *You've found us out.* Are you trying to make my life miserable? *Of course, that's exactly what we're doing.* You and Dad aren't like other parents—you're too old-fashioned. *What can we say? We're overachievers.* Are you trying to ruin my teenage years? *Absolutely. We stay awake thinking of ways we can ruin your life.*[2]

Then it dawned on me. It all made sense now. We were living out our own episode of Mutual of Omaha's *Wild Kingdom*, the *Animal Planet* of my generation.

When I was little, my family gathered on Sunday nights to watch episodes of *Wild Kingdom*. Sitting on our brown shag carpet in front of the television, I recall watching a white fluffy polar bear cub suckling on a proud new mama polar bear. As mama bear tenderly cared for her baby cub the scene faded to black, leading us to believe, as the credits rolled, all was perfect in their polar bear world. What *Wild Kingdom* host Marlin Perkins didn't produce was a follow-up episode sixteen years later when papa polar bear would have regretted not eating baby cub when he had the chance—a frightening similarity to life in our home.

**About the time my first baby became a teenager,
I wondered if I needed "love your teenager"
hormone replacement therapy.**

Where was our dimpled cherub? Who had replaced her with this self-centered, me-me-me creature? A human being who felt only her needs, her wants, her pain, and her pleasure.

When the Lord put a family sabbatical on my heart, you can imagine how eager I was to share the news with my teenage daughter. But before you get the idea my teenager is just a self-centered me-me-me creature, you must understand she learned a few bad habits from the best of the best. Her mother.

Selfishness Is Genetic

Selfishness is a genetic trait I passed down to Meghan, just like her button nose and the mole behind her left ear. I understand this trait was passed down from the very first two people God created. When we want what we want and put self first, a selfish-seed is planted. If this seed is not immediately killed with spiritual weed-killer—God's Word—a mighty oak of selfishness can take up residency in the heart.

God is pretty clear about what the unselfish look like. Jesus is our perfect example. His Word says:

Let nothing be done through selfish ambition or conceit, but in lowliness of mind let each esteem others better than himself. Let each of you look out not only for his own interests, but also for the interests of others. Let this mind be in you which was also in Christ Jesus, who, being in the form of God, did not consider it robbery to be equal with God, but made Himself of no reputation, taking the form of a bondservant, and coming in the likeness of men. (Philippians 2:3-7)

One of my most disturbing parenting memories was born of my selfish nature. Philippians 2 would have been a great help to me when

I was a younger mom. The way I responded to some me-time gone awry was a clear sign my selfish nature was at an all-time high.

With four little ones at home, I was in desperate need of a day at the salon. My hair was a mess, and I drooled over the opportunity to have it cut and styled. When the opportunity arose, I leapt like a matted-hair ballerina at the chance. Marking off the days on my calendar, I joyfully anticipated the moments I would spend sitting in a chair while the stylist massaged delicious smelling shampoo onto my head and rinsed my soapy locks with warm, pulsating water. Heaven.

The day arrived for my hair appointment. I had finished homework with the children and was busy making spaghetti. I worked out the timing perfectly. The food was just about on the table. Paul would be walking in the front door any minute and I'd be running out. Then the phone rang.

"Hi, cutie, what are you doing?" *He sounded way too nice.*

"I'm getting dinner on the table. Where are you?"

"I don't know how to say this. I know you were looking forward to having your hair done, but I'm going to be late tonight."

Did he just say what I think he said?

Was he feeding white rice to starving children? Had he just rescued a family of kittens from a burning building? To a woman in self-mode, reasons don't really matter, and there isn't one that's ever good enough. Whatever reason he gave I didn't hear. I was livid. All I heard was what sounded like static on a poorly tuned-in radio station.

The memories I have after hanging up the phone are a blur. How I wish the Lord would remove the ones I do have from my mind, but He hasn't. Just like the apostle Paul's thorn, God knows how the uncomfortable and sometimes painful memories of my failures as a mom have kept me humble over the years. What I will tell you is this: when spaghetti sauce in a bowl is slammed down at a velocity that could break the speed of sound, it has an Old Faithful geyser effect and can shoot twelve feet in the air.

Once my tantrum was over it looked as if a scene from CSI had been shot in my kitchen.

Sadly, Meghan has the best recollection of her mother coming unhinged with Paul Newman's Original Sauce. And now, with my idea of a radical sabbatical, I was being selfish once again. Asking my daughter to stop all of her after-school activities wasn't something she was happy about. After all, she was quite comfortable with her busyness; it was her selfish mom's discomfort over driving everyone everywhere that began our activity-fast. So why was she the one suffering?

Meghan's Letter to Me

Meghan is all grown up and attending a Christian college in Southern California. Our beautiful overachiever skipped a grade to begin The Master's College this fall as a junior, at the ripe old age of eighteen. I thought I'd share with you a letter she wrote to me recently about yours truly and her radical sabbatical experience:

Dear Mom,

It's early in the morning as I reach back into my own memory, bringing forth our radical sabbatical and the lessons I learned so long ago.

It was New Year's Eve, and I was ecstatic to be with family friends rather than staying home, which promised a much earlier bedtime. While I was engaging myself with my friends, you began to concoct an idea that was to begin in a mere couple of hours. I was oblivious to your thoughts as you received support from Dad, felt questioning from yourself, and set your mind to twist our lives around. But truthfully, Mom, if I knew your radical plans I probably wouldn't have thought much about it.

Because early on New Year's Day when you and Dad called a family meeting after our devotion, I thought this was another of your little phases. Like the lemonade stand you painted and we used once or the move we were going to make to Texas or the family trip we were supposed to take to Washington D.C. that never materialized. I wasn't worried. Yep, this was a phase.

You would break down in the spring when we signed up for soccer; there was no way you were going to cut my weekly singing lessons. You were Mom. The nice one. We went to you with cut knees and broken little hearts. You made yummy dinners and talked to Dad in the late hours of the night if he was too hard on us. And yet somehow your creative mind, usually used for good, warped with exhaustion and spun out your radical sabbatical.

You didn't change your mind. We learned that extremely fast. And our activities as a family changed quickly. Our ice skating escapade was an exhausting, expensive wreck. We suffered through Daffodil Hill. However, we also turned our fingers all colors of purple and blue as we picked berries. We had movie nights filled with laughter and long car rides discovering the town we grew up in. I found out that Dad was pretty funny, and I wouldn't die if my hand brushed by David's in the car. I learned sharing drinks with my siblings wasn't poisonous and school friends weren't always the best.

I find it funny that my hardest year in high school was the year of the radical sabbatical. I cried for the first time at school after the experience of a fire-spitting bully. I found myself with an overwhelming crush on a boy who simply liked the idea of being liked, and I lost my best girlfriend to a young man she found more important than me.

I think that during our sabbatical year you held me more than you had in quite a while, allowing your arms to run with hot tears and shirts to soak with salty heartbreak. Now that I think about it, our year-long sabbatical experiment not only taught me about being too busy but about my mom. I was no longer too busy, but now I had time to see who you really were.

As a parent you have had an immeasurable impact on me. Not only do I look like you and make your facial expressions, but I dream like you and think like you. Your lessons spanning from simple childhood "do this" and "don't do that" of stealing and sharing to how to treat others who are different than me with the love of God and form honoring relationships have stuck with me. Each tidbit of advice from sidelong whispers to messages on Facebook have glued themselves to my psyche. Your words have never died in my heart. If I disagree or disobey, they are still there, sticking like sharp pins and hot needles.

Now, Mom, your words get to affect others. The advice I get for free is going to have a price tag on it and sit on a shelf. I am so proud of you and that I get to call you "Mom." Your life has taught me so much and helped create the person I am now. I might struggle and give in to the urges of the young, but you're always somewhere in my mind. You have done well, if I do say so myself.

Our sabbatical taught me I can enjoy my life rather than allow busyness to drive it away. Thank you for giving me this lesson so young. I will be able to one day love my husband and spend time with my children and be able to guard myself from being painfully selfish. If you knew the way I felt about you then—and the way I feel about you now—I am sure you would be encouraged. I remember telling people if I had only one child I wanted a girl. You know why? Because I wanted to be a mom, a confidante, to someone in the same way you were to me. One of my biggest dreams is to be like you.

Love,

Meghan

Meghan was fifteen years old when we began our radical sabbatical year. She was involved in voice lessons, soccer, community theatre, and choir. Letting these go wasn't easy for her or me. As I shared earlier with you, she was the child who had the biggest breakthrough.

These were her words in November of our experimental year that surprised me with her change of attitude, "Mom, why don't we just stay home and hang out as a family this weekend. Let's stay in our pjs and watch movies together."

Our teenager had gone from not wanting anything to do with her siblings, or our sabbatical, to being the first to suggest a relaxing family day at home together.

It took ten months to see a change. But the change in her was well worth the wait.

Dear Lord, my teen is a tough nut to crack. Help me guide my almost-adult children on a path that leads to you. Show me ways I can curb their passion for busyness. Bring to mind ways I can change too. Help me be a parent who isn't selfish but takes time for the right things. And please remind me every day that you've created me to tread water longer than my teenager can make it rain. In Jesus' name I pray. Amen.

- Take an hour to sit and talk with your teenager.
- Try to listen without lecturing.
- Ask your teenager to mark a day on the calendar for the two of you. Share a burger, grab a hot chocolate, or go for a long walk together.
- Don't be surprised if your teen doesn't want to spend time with you. Encourage it anyway. Time together is a must for parents and teens. Mark a date on your calendar today. They'll survive, and so will you.

WHAT HILLS ARE YOU DYING ON?

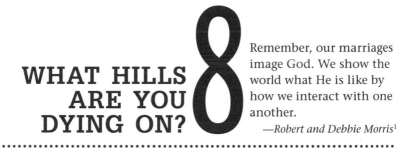

Remember, our marriages image God. We show the world what He is like by how we interact with one another.
—*Robert and Debbie Morris*[1]

Recently, I overheard Grace sharing with her friend, "My parents met in a graveyard behind a soda machine." I had to chuckle to myself. She was partly right. My husband and I met over a homicide. Romantic, isn't it? He was a police officer and I was a police dispatcher, and we worked the graveyard shift together. Anyone who knows Paul and me knows our "How did you meet?" story is far from picture perfect, but the Lord had plans for us.

It was New Year's Eve when our department received a 911 call telling us someone ran into a motel lobby and crouched down behind a soda machine. At two in the morning in a seedy part of town, the employee making the 911 call refused to leave her enclosed bullet-proof office to check on this stranger. Once the police arrived, they soon discovered the young man had been shot numerous times after a drug deal had gone bad.

Paul arrived on the scene with his beat partner and was given the task of taking the homicide report. This included coming into dispatch later to take statements from dispatchers like me. Both of us were in our twenties and pretty wet behind the ears. Young police department newbies like us worked the weekend graveyard shift. There is a bond that grows when you work shootings, gang fights, and homicides together.

Over the years, Paul's beat partner and friend had been shot three times in three separate incidents. I was thankful when Paul's life journey took him to law school and off the streets. No longer would I have to argue with him over a police radio, "One-frank-eleven I'm sending you a cover unit," only to hear Paul reply, "I'm Code 4," which translated means: Leave me alone, Joanne. I'm fine.

We enjoyed working in a paramilitary environment. Both of us are the oldest in our families, and we both quite often see things in black and white, a sometimes lethal combination for police work and parenting. I do believe our working relationship gave us the fortitude to complete a radical sabbatical. Our children like to tell people, "Dad is the Old Testament and Mom is the New Testament." Paul has no problem laying down the law, while I give them a big helping of grace.

If my husband and I were rated the same way we rate our kids, Paul would be a head-kid and I'd be a heart-kid. So it was no surprise when I came up with the sabbatical idea and Paul went running with it. Out of my heart, my emotional state of mind told me time was slipping away and we only had one shot at these young family years. Paul, on the other hand, made a logical decision. Taking time off would be good. Peace instead of chaos would be good. Eating out less would be good—especially for our bank account. (*Finances are figured in his head no matter what we are doing, another endearing trait of his. Cue heavy sarcasm.*)

When I struggled in the beginning of our sabbatical about how it would look to our friends and family, Paul didn't worry about that at all. He has no problem whatsoever standing for what he believes in. Probably one of the reasons we are the only house in our neighborhood with a twenty-foot flagpole out front. "We are the greatest country in the world. It's a time of war, Joanne. You should be happy Home Depot was out of the forty-foot poles."

"I'm not embarrassed to fly the flag, Paul. It's just that the houses on our street are so close together, and no one else seems to have a flagpole right out in front of the house. I'm afraid if we put a light on top of it planes might land in our driveway."

"Well, maybe our neighbors will take their patriotic cue from us. We can be the house that leads by example."

He was right. I stood beside him as he painted the pole white, and I quietly bent down with a sharp rock in hand and carved "Psalm 33:12" in the wet cement.[2]

This sabbatical is supposed to be about the kids, *not us*.

Paul and I both understand the importance of a strong marriage. This is one of the reasons we invest in attending annual marriage conferences and lead weekly marriage studies in our home. We believe wholeheartedly that a family is only as strong as the marriage within it. How we treat one another will set the standard for our children's marriages.

What our children see in our marriage today, we will see tomorrow in theirs.

While running from one activity to the next, there were many weekends we saw very little of one another—both taking off in different directions with children in tow. Our sabbatical gave our marriage a deep sigh of relief. We looked forward to more time together, just the two of us.

Looking back, spare time gave us the ability to focus on areas in our marriage we had neglected. Our sabbatical from busyness gave me the opportunity to see, painfully, where I needed to grow as a wife. A wife can learn a lot about her marriage in twelve months. Our radical sabbatical taught me a great lesson about what hills were worth dying on one evening when we were out to dinner with friends. That same year I was also schooled in having great expectations in my husband that weren't all that great.

I was raised by a U.S. Marine. I'm the oldest of four children and find leadership roles enjoyable. I'm the person you would lean on if you needed a shoulder to cry on. I'm the friend you would call if you wanted someone on your side, and I'm the mother who demands respect and tolerates nothing less. As you can imagine, as a newly married woman, I was a real peach. Though I didn't drink the women's lib Kool-Aid, I would still challenge my husband regularly. C'mon, I was the daughter of a hard-chargin' Marine. There wasn't a hill I wouldn't die on.

"Why are you paying the bills that way?" "Why am *I* putting gas in the car again?" "Are you seriously going to wear that shirt?" "We should leave for your parents' house earlier than that." "Why did you tell him no—I just told him yes." I would challenge Paul's answers on almost any of the above. On and on it went until one fateful evening and a dinner for four.

After making some new friends, the more intimate we became the more I began to notice a few things. My new friend challenged her husband on just about everything he said or did. No matter how inconsequential, whenever her husband spoke, he was interrupted. "Sweetheart, you're wrong, that's not what she said." "Why are you having lasagna? You told me you were in the mood for a steak." "The kids were five and three, not six and four."

What I witnessed that evening broke my heart. This poor man was being nitpicked to death. The hills my girlfriend was dying on were pathetic speed bumps. I tried to convince myself the hills I died on with Paul were much more important than my friend's at dinner. Unfortunately, I couldn't shake the feeling that I was looking into a full-length mirror.

Then it came to me, the story in the Bible where God hands out the consequences to Adam and Eve's sin. "He said to the woman, 'I will sharpen the pain of your pregnancy, and in pain you will give birth. And you will desire to control your husband, but he will rule over you'" (Genesis 3:16 NLT).

If you didn't catch that last line back there, let me remind you again: *and you will desire to control your husband, but he will rule over you.*

The desire to nitpick, nag, and control goes all the way back to the garden of Eden. Challenging and manipulating my husband is part of my sinful nature. Once I'd been reminded, my need to win each battle and fight to the death on every hill was something I had to deal with spiritually, the real fight was on. I refused to let my carnal nature win out. I began taking my irritations and wrongful desires to the cross.

Each day, I prayed for the Lord to open my eyes to what really mattered. My marriage legacy was to encourage my husband, not discourage him. I made a point to try to keep my challenges in the privacy of our bedroom, far away from prying little eyes and ears. I especially didn't want my daughters to learn any bad habits from me. I knew my marriage faux pas could have a long reach into my children's marriages.

The change in our home was miraculous. The hot-button issues I stood up for at any cost soon became almost silly to defend or debate. I discovered I wasn't as frustrated or as irritable anymore. I realized taking charge was not mine to take. God gave the leadership role to my husband years ago when I said, "I do." My constant challenges were a direct insult to the very One who had given him this position in our home.

Today, after our sabbatical, I refuse to die on any insignificant battlefields. The only bloody battles fought these days are by the sword of the Spirit, though I still take a hit for the team every now and again. This daughter of a U.S. Marine is finally learning to stand down and let her husband take his rightful place in the home.[3]

My Expectations Aren't Always God's Expectations

Great expectations—more than the title of a literary classic. My great expectations were also the burden buried in the deepest recesses of my marriage. Most often, the problem became *great* when I expected Paul to do something I would do in the same situation. I have suffered many years from great expectations and the conflicts attached to them.

My great expectations like to rear their ugly heads during special occasions. Because I enjoy giving thoughtful gifts as tokens of my affection, I expect my husband to do the same. And during our sabbatical, without outside activities to take up my every moment, I had time to focus on my marriage expectations like a heat-seeking missile.

It was my birthday, and I couldn't wait to open my gift from Paul. I *expected* it to be stupendous. After all, I'd given him clues about what I wanted for weeks. When the time came to open up my gift, instead of the gardening tools, books, or CDs I had suggested I would love, my husband gave me a chalkboard with a bit of French flair. Not only was there no place to hang this in my kitchen, I didn't have anything French in my home, nor had I ever asked for anything French, or even chalky for that matter.

Realizing he had not hit a grand slam in the gift-giving department that evening, my husband nervously blurted out this item was purchased half-off at a drugstore on his way home from work—that night. Big mistake.

I had a flashback.

Mother's Day 2001, I'd given birth to our fourth child six weeks earlier. I *expected* a bounty of gifts from my husband. After all, I'd just given him a ten pound son. That morning, our three older children, ages two through nine, filed into my bedroom to give me a kiss. Climbing into bed with me, they whispered, "Daddy didn't take us to get you anything for Mother's Day."

Being a postpartum ball of hormones, you can imagine my response. The plant I was given later that afternoon was purchased from a man on a street corner who tried to give him a deal on a Harley Davidson throw rug.

The next year, when Christmas rolled around, I knew better than to hint about anything. This time I would tell him *specifically* what I wanted. My gift of choice—a delicate, sparkly, cross necklace. It didn't have to be made of diamonds, it just had to be delicate *and* sparkly *and* a cross. Instead, I received a necklace with a Frisbee-sized lighthouse in a heart, with the birthstones of our children placed inside.

I have never liked lighthouses. I know some people love them, but I don't. As a matter of fact, the ocean frightens me. *See chapter 1—I don't like to swim, remember?* I expected Paul to know that. But I knew he had tried this time to be thoughtful, so there were no tears. What mom wouldn't appreciate something with her children's birthstones in it? Still, if I'm ever in Las Vegas, I know this necklace will be coveted by many Elvis-impersonating, hairy-chested men.

During our sabbatical I had more time to pray for my husband.

**Prayer has a way of clearing the cobwebs
of selfish expectations from my heart.**

I was reminded that my husband works two jobs so I can stay home with our children. His concerns are mortgage payments, college tuition, and medical bills. My concerns include how much milk we have in the fridge, did the kids finish their homework, and whether or not my black necklace works with my grey-striped shirt.

My husband allows me the freedom to pursue my God-given passion of writing and has encouraged me to follow every dream I have ever had, regardless of how monumental or insignificant. He regularly watches our children so I can attend writers' groups, teach women's Bible studies, and speak at conferences. He tells me I'm beautiful, calls me several times every day just to see how I'm doing, and has never once used a foul word in anger toward me. He never gets upset over dust bunnies, soap scum in the shower, or that I sign him up for things at church—which I do quite often.

I discovered expectations are kind of like when we take a drink of something expecting one thing but get something else. Have you ever done that? I recently picked up my cup in our kitchen, thinking it held milk, and got a mouthful of orange juice instead. It was awful. Because I expected milk, I missed out on the sweet swallow of orange juice. It made me wonder, *How much have I missed because I expect things to be the way I want them?*

After quite a few years of marriage, my expectations have changed. I no longer expect my husband to bring me joy. This is God's job, not his. I no longer believe happiness comes in the form of gifts. My husband brings me joy and happiness in so many other ways. Those are the things I try to focus on when Valentine's Day and Christmas roll around. I now look forward to the joy of the simple things, like taking a drive and holding hands, walking to the coffee shop and reading the newspaper, sharing lunch together, or watching a movie snuggled up on the couch.

As I've learned not to *expect*, I've been blessed with abundance. Things such as joy, contentment, and peace all come much easier now. No longer manufactured by Hallmark or the obligatory reason, I've removed the burden of great expectations from the shoulders of my precious husband, and I've been pleasantly surprised by the unexpected.

Dear Lord, you know the places in our relationship where we need the most help. Help us to have a marriage our children want to emulate one day. I want them to experience a home where we take time for one another, laugh together, and love one another. Help us leave a marriage legacy that points our future generations to you. In Jesus' name I pray. Amen.

- What hills are you dying on? Do they have eternal value? If they don't, retreat from the battlefield.
- Ask the Lord if your expectations for your husband are His expectations for your husband. Release your spouse from all unrealistic expectations today.

- Pray for your husband daily. Make a point to ask him before he leaves for work how you can pray for him.
- Hire a sitter and surprise your husband with lunch at work. Or send the kids to your friend's house for a few hours and make him a special dinner at home—for just the two of you.

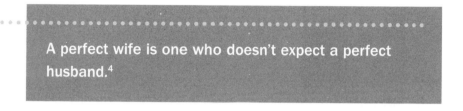

A perfect wife is one who doesn't expect a perfect husband.[4]

PART III

Beware

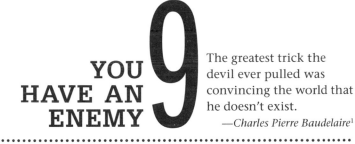

YOU HAVE AN ENEMY

The greatest trick the devil ever pulled was convincing the world that he doesn't exist.

—*Charles Pierre Baudelaire*[1]

The Exorcist ranks as the highest grossing horror movie and was named scariest movie of all time by *Entertainment Weekly*.[2] Filmed in 1973, long before computer-generated effects, the production crew worked with a small budget and cast quite a few no-name actors. The question remains: why would a horror movie decades old reign supreme as the scariest film of all time?

Answer: *The Exorcist* is about the devil. This movie scares us to our core because Satan exists. He is real, and he is alive—and in the deepest parts of our soul we know it.

Our radical sabbatical opened my eyes to lots of things, including the role the devil played in keeping us in a constant state of busy. The bondage of my busyness was most often due to my self-induced choices, but there was one who enjoyed watching me struggle with my captivity of activity and smiled with twisted pleasure the more difficult life became.

Many people admit to having no relationship with Jesus Christ. Yet I find it interesting that so many of these same people are fascinated by television shows and documentaries about mediums, ghosts, and psychics. They give their attention to darkness and the evil one who wishes them failure, heartache, destruction, and bondage, yet refuse to inquire about the one true light of the world:

the only one who has the power to bring freedom and peace from the emptiness and chaos of life.

Could it be they find it safer knowing Satan is real and are more afraid of discovering Jesus is real? If they came to realize Jesus is more real and alive than the dark forces in the movies and documentaries they consume, they would have to make a choice to either accept or deny Christ. And, quite often, our pride won't let us do that.

B.U.S.Y.

My girlfriend had just gotten home from a women's conference and called to share what she'd learned. Since we don't live close to one another anymore, we enjoy taking notes and encouraging each other with our new spiritual discoveries.

"I learned an acronym for busy—Burdened Under Satan's Yoke," she excitedly shared.

"What a perfect definition," I replied. I had been living under Satan's yoke of busy, that's for sure.

A yoke is a piece of curved timber placed over the neck of oxen to join them together. When oxen work the fields yoked together, one oxen bears the heaviest burden, and no matter how difficult the burden, there is no getting away from the other.

Satan presses the yoke on our necks as he leads us with cords of falsehood and ties of lies. —*Beth Moore*[3]

Another definition for *yoke* is "bondage or slavery." Whether or not I wanted to admit it, I had yoked myself to busyness. I was enslaved to my activities, and my burden was far from light.

With the phone still in the crook of my neck, I flipped through the pages in my Bible. Scouring the gospel of Matthew, I needed to be reminded of what God's yoke was like. "Come to Me, all you who labor and are heavy laden, and I will give you rest. Take My yoke upon you and learn from Me, for I am gentle and lowly in heart, and you will find rest for your souls. For My yoke is easy and My burden is light" (Matthew 11:28-30). Those words were refreshing to read. So much so that I made the decision to read them every time I felt painfully burdened.

Did you realize you have an enemy? Not very comforting, is it? You do. He is alive at this very moment with your face on his most-wanted list. Satan makes Adolf Hitler look like SpongeBob Squarepants. Proudly bearing the title Father of Lies, he hopes to convince you that you're a failure. He loves to use busyness as a tool to hold you in bondage by its distracting power, and he would love nothing more than to mortally wound your marriage, your relationships—your life.

God's Word tells us Satan roams the earth like a hungry lion, to and fro, searching for someone to destroy. Jesus warns us he is real. He tells us Satan's purpose is to steal from us, kill us, and destroy us. But Jesus ends His warning with His good news.

The thief does not come except to steal, and to kill, and to destroy. I have come that they may have life, and that they may have it more abundantly. (John 10:10)

**Busyness is part of Satan's three-step plan.
He uses it as a weapon to steal our time, kill our joy,
and destroy our relationships.**

The Enemy Is a Thief

Some of the best thieves in the world consider their illegal preoccupation a profession. Taking their work seriously, they have a goal and a plan to succeed in mind. They learn as much as they can about their victims to discover weaknesses. Their goal is to find the soft underbelly of their prey, a vulnerable place where they can breech security—all for the sake of taking something that was never theirs in the first place.

Satan works the same way.

God's Word says the enemy of our souls is a thief. He steals. Time is where his plan unfolds. He steals moments from us that we have no way of getting back, especially time with our families. He delights in averting our eyes to distract us from Jesus and cause us to focus on the cares of the world. Once time is stolen, anger and resentment aren't far off, and regret settles in to torment us.

Time stealers come in all shapes and sizes. They are Satan's favorite tools of the trade. Television, talking on the phone, exercise, shopping, and even our jobs can become time stealers. For me, the greatest time stealer is my computer. I can get lost for hours traveling down the Internet's bunny hole. Blogging, Facebook, Twitter, e-mail, all things I can justify for good reasons. It's not long before the computer becomes the time stealing felon of my day. Satan finds joy in my unproductive busyness.

When the kids began complaining about my laptop being open all the time, I spoke with my husband about it. He confirmed their accusations. *Whose side was he on, anyway?* We came up with a way for me to get my work done and enjoy some Internet playtime too. Now I close my laptop from 3 P.M. to 8:30 P.M. That way it's off when the children run in the front door from school and can go back on once they are tucked in bed.

A good way to find out if you have a time stealer is to look back at the end of your day and write down all you've accomplished.

You will struggle with a list of daily accomplishments when there's a time stealer in your life.

The Enemy Is a Murderer

God says the enemy of our souls kills. He is a murderer. Once he steals our time, he kills our joy. When the enemy succeeds at stealing moments, hours, and days from our lives, he takes a kill-shot at our joy. He should be on death row for murdering innumerable joyful days meant to build a strong foundation for our families.

Have you ever experienced the joy of the Lord? No, I'm not talking about happiness. Happiness is not the same at all. Happiness relies solely on the external. Things like pleasure, personal experience, and circumstance. The joy of the Lord is wholly different. Let me give you a few examples. Chocolate peanut butter ice cream makes me happy. Blue jeans that fit make me happy. Children who don't argue in the car make me happy. But smiling while I'm grieving, being able to hug someone who has hurt me, and having indescribable peace when my world is falling apart—now that is the joy of the Lord.

I want joy in my life. I want joy in my home, and I want it in my relationships. The joy of the Lord is what separates Christians from the rest of the world. It is where our grace-filled rubber meets the road, if you will. Being a regular Sunday pew warmer will not build your spiritual muscles. Sure, it's a great start, but having peace through a storm, a song in your heart through a fiery trial, or the strength to get up the very next day when your heart is breaking— that is a reflection of the joy of the Lord.

I witnessed the joy of the Lord last night.

Friends of ours pastor a church. They built their little church from the ground up more than twenty-five years ago. Slanderous words, hurtful accusations, and unbearable gossip have been the arrows used to pierce their hearts.

Instead of putting their congregation through months of ugliness, our friends decided to step down. In return, the Lord blessed them and opened a path for them to move close to their children and grandchildren but far away from us. It was an honor to be part of their going-away potluck. What could easily have turned into an evening of mourning was instead filled with fellowship, laughter, and many stories of God's faithfulness. As we arrived, they were full of smiles and hugs, letting us know they were waiting with joyful anticipation for what God has planned next for their lives.

The joy of the Lord makes all the difference. A friend once shared with me, "A mom sets the thermostat in her home." A poor attitude or sulky pout from me sets the tone for the day in my home. Each morning I have one more chance to create a dwelling place for my children where laughter and love are the primary building blocks for joy.

The Enemy Is a Destroyer

Fifty percent of all marriages end in divorce. The majority of children raised in a Christian home will walk away from their faith in college. More single women are having children today than married women. These staggering statistics have been floating around for years.

The enemy is working overtime. Once he kills our time and kills our joy, he moves on to destroy our relationships.

I have a friend who works long hours. Her time is filled with her job and her children, and her husband gets the few leftover minutes in her day. She shared with me how little she has to say to him and that they don't laugh together like they used to. She feels life has become a to-do list and he is just another task to check off. At this rate, it won't be long before the enemy laughs at yet another destroyed relationship.

Abundant Life

The Lord came into our world to give us abundant life. When I think of abundance, I sometimes put my eyes on the tangible material things that bring me comfort and pleasure—a new car or a bulging bank account. That kind of thinking trips me up.

The abundant life is not made up of financial ease, perfect relationships, nor is it problem-free. The abundant life Jesus is talking about is an abundant *spiritual* life—a life full of Him and His every spiritual trait: forgiveness, mercy, grace, thankfulness, love, joy, peace, patience, kindness, goodness, faithfulness, gentleness, and self-control. You can't buy the abundant life on Amazon or Craigslist.

Ask a mother whose adult children aren't speaking to each other what she would pay for peace. Ask someone who is going through a divorce what he or she would pay for forgiveness. Ask a person who is morbidly obese what he or she would pay for self-control.

Jesus promises to give us an abundance of everything we need to get through each day successfully in this world, including the battle of busyness. If you had told me eleven years ago I'd be writing a book, I would have laughed. If you had told me that I would be writing a book with the name of Jesus anywhere between the front and back cover, I would have snorted.

God loves to use the foolish things of the world to confound the wise. Thankfully, I am more foolish than most. If I've learned anything in my walk of faith, it's that Jesus Christ is real, He is alive, and His Word is true. So when He says He came into the world to give me an abundant life, I believe Him.

The enemy comes to steal, kill, and destroy, but Christ came so we could have life more abundantly. If I'm feeling unbearably burdened, it is not coming from Him. His burdens are light. His yoke is easy.

Dear Lord, thank you for warning me in your Word about the one seeking to destroy me. Help me give Satan as little attention as possible but as much as I should. Because of you there's truly nothing to fear. Help me to be on guard for any time stealers in my day. Remind me that joy is a choice. Fill me with every quality of you, so I can live out my days with an abundant life. In Jesus' name I pray. Amen.

- Make a list of the time stealers in your life.
- What is the temperature of your home today? Set it on joy and leave it there.
- Spend time in prayer. Ask God for His spiritual abundance in your life.
- What burden are you yoked to? Give it to the Lord and ask Him to make it light.

THE ATTRACTION OF DISTRACTION

10

> Among the enemies to devotion, none is so harmful as distractions.
>
> —*A. W. Tozer*[1]

"But it's soooooo beautiful," yells the mosquito, distracted by the bug zapper in the movie *A Bug's Life*. Ignoring the warnings of his mosquito friend, we see him flying in a trance, distracted from his original course. As we watch in cartoon horror, he flies directly into the beautiful shiny bright light and is zapped.

I am that mosquito.

I'm easily distracted. Just ask my husband. My nickname is Bright Shiny Thing. It's true. Whatever I begin, no matter how simple, I end up off-course. *Distract* means "to draw away from or divert." No matter what is on my to-do list for the day, I am constantly diverted.

When I think of distractions, I think of how I'm drawn to the television anytime it's on or how a call from a girlfriend can derail me from my plans to clean the kitchen. Where busyness is concerned, distractions aren't always things we can turn off or hang up. Distractions can begin as good things too.

The Fine Art of Distraction

When I became a mother, I went from being the *distractee* to the *distractor*. It was during these early years of parenting that I learned the fine art of distraction. Today I hold an advanced degree in the field. When my first child was an infant, I hated to hear her cry. I wanted to soothe every wail and quiet every whimper. My mother encouraged me, "It's OK for her to cry, Joanne. It strengthens her lungs." *Really? Where does it say that in the medical books?* I wondered.

As she grew, when she'd reach for something I didn't want her to have, I'd tell her no. If that didn't work, I began the amazing game of distraction. "Meghan, look over here." I'd shake her favorite toy, drawing her eyes away from whatever was holding her attention. By the time child number four came into the world, I was a master of distraction.

I fine-tuned my skill at the grocery store, drawing my children away from the cookie, soda pop, and candy aisles, and anything that whirled or whistled by them at the check-out counter. I distracted with the finesse and speed of a gazelle. My children had the attention spans of gnats, cutting their focus down to mini-moments. "Look here. See what I have? Oh, wow! Come check this out!"

In my own life, distraction was the very first step toward discontentment. Quite honestly, when I'm no longer content with the uncountable blessings I've already been given, my day loses its sparkle.

Distractions of the Mind

Discontentment makes way for grumbling, and grumbling establishes a wide path for discontentment to take up residency in my heart. My mind likes to work overtime as I scrub and wipe, polish and sweep. Soon it wanders to the Land of Grumbling and Fables.

Cheryl has it easy. Her husband does the dishes for her every night. Truth: Cheryl's husband did it once on Cheryl's fortieth birthday.

Terry's teenage daughter was cleaning the kitchen when I was over last. Her daughter is so helpful. Truth: Terry's teenage daughter was cleaning the kitchen because she was being disciplined for coming home late the night before.

Melanie gets to work all day with adults. Truth: Melanie would give anything to cut back her hours at work, and she can't stand half the adults in her office.

All I do is clean, clean, clean. I'm just the maid around here! Truth: I spend more time each day checking my e-mail than I spend cleaning the kitchen.

A word of hard-gained wisdom: If I had made an about-face from the Land of Grumbling and Fables and sprinted back to truth, I could have avoided many an ugly outburst.

Distractions led to discontentment, which gave a green light to covetousness, and God commanded us against that. He ended his list of ten with it. "You shall not covet your neighbor's wife; and you shall not desire your neighbor's house, his field, his male servant, his female servant, his ox, his donkey, or anything that is your neighbor's" (Deuteronomy 5:21). That includes my neighbor's dishwashing husband and my friend's adult-time at the office.

When God created me, He knew how much I would struggle with distraction and discontentment. These were the two specialized tools used to sculpt my heart to covet. And when I became a willful participant in any of the above, I sinned before the Lord.

My husband has a real estate broker's license, and sometimes I accompany him when he's viewing homes that have come on the market that are unoccupied. We climb into our car, pick up a coffee, and begin our adventure. As we wind our way around the beautiful Sierra Nevada foothills, we stop and look at vacant houses.

Looking at beautiful homes with exquisite kitchens is not always the best choice for a woman who suffers from granite countertop and double-oven envy. Later, when I come home to my gummy-sock-grey tile, my heart covets, telling God loud and clear that

I am not grateful for the blessings I've received. Dangerous ground to be on.

Busyness Distracts

It's impossible to write a book about how to break free from busyness without sharing the Bible's poster gal of busyness herself, Martha. Yes, Martha and the Proverbs 31 Woman might as well be sisters of pain when it comes to hitting me right between the eyes.

My name is Joanne, and I'm a Martha. I am a Type A, do-do-do queen with a quirk. I'm easily distracted by the mundane and microscopic. I volunteer for too much, am soon distracted by the overwhelming nature of the task, and within minutes I'm irritable over the unimportant and soon angry that no one is helping me. Sound like a Martha to you?

When I took the time to study Martha, I discovered there are only five teeny-tiny verses in the gospel of Luke that share her story, yet five verses pack a knock-out punch, don't they?

While teaching at a recent women's conference, I shared how the Lord gave me another insight into Martha; surprisingly, it wasn't about her busyness.

Now it happened as they went that He entered a certain village; and a certain woman named Martha welcomed Him into her house. And she had a sister called Mary, who also sat at Jesus' feet and heard His word. But Martha was distracted with much serving, and she approached Him and said, "Lord, do You not care that my sister has left me to serve alone? Therefore tell her to help me." And Jesus answered and said to her, "Martha, Martha, you are worried and troubled about many things. But one thing is needed, and Mary has chosen that good part, which will not be taken away from her." (Luke 10:38-42)

The Distracted Miss Out

We see Martha quite a few times throughout the Gospels, much of the time she is serving. But in Luke 10 she is not only serving but also distracted—drawn away from or diverted from that which was most important. Not only is Martha busy, busy, busy, but she is being taken away from the best part of her day, her time with Jesus.

When Paul wrote his first letter to the Corinthians, he felt concentrating on one's time with the Lord was important enough to share with them: "And this I say for your own profit, not that I may put a leash on you, but for what is proper, and that you may serve the Lord without distraction" (1 Corinthians 7:35).

As much as I enjoy serving Him through women's Bible studies, writing, and encouraging friends, I must ask the Lord every morning what His better choice for my day is. Time with Him is a blessed opportunity. I've discovered the more I spend time with Him, the more I want to spend time with Him. The better choice lesson can often sting, especially when I examine the way I've spent my day.

The last time I read these five verses, the Lord didn't emphasize the lesson of the better choice; rather, He opened my eyes to how many things I miss when I am distracted.

It was a Saturday morning and David was pitching for his little league baseball team. I decided to forego his game that morning to stay home to make potato salad for his team party that would be held later in the afternoon. I couldn't count how many times I'd sat in bleachers or on the sidelines to watch my son play his baseball. I was his number one fan.

Would you believe that on this Saturday morning my little boy hit a home run? His one and only home run. It had never happened before, and it hasn't happened since. While I busied myself, distracted in my kitchen making potato salad I could have easily bought at the store, my little boy rounded the bases to rousing cheers, minus one voice—mine.

How many special moments have I missed because I was distracted? What good things have I added to my to-do list that drew me away from the best things God has for me?

David's home run was a moment I'll never get back. How many other moments has God had something for me I've missed? I'm thankful the Lord is so gracious and loving that He hasn't allowed me to be privy to all of them.

Priority Distractions

You would think a master of distraction would know when she's being distracted. Unfortunately, that's not always the case. I recall a time when I had three children at home under the age of seven and became immensely distracted.

For the first time, I was able to be a full-time, stay-at-home mom. Buried in a sea of everything small, I lost sight of my priorities. I can't tell you exactly how it happened, but I was convinced there must be more important things for me to do than wipe little bums and even littler noses. In a matter of hours my distraction became discontentment, followed by a big dose of coveting. I just knew my girlfriends at work were doing more important and valuable things. *They* were really making a difference in the world.

At the time, Paul was working nights and going to law school during the day. *Surely he would agree I needed an outside interest to bring me a bit of joy and value as a person. What if it also brings in a little extra spending money? Of course, he'll be on board.*

But, just to play it safe, I wasn't going to say a word until my cottage business stock was selling publicly.

Walking him to the front door, I handed him his lunch and kissed him good-bye. He bent down and kissed the toddler on my hip before leaving. He suddenly turned back to me. "Joanne, I almost forgot. I need you to call the newspaper today. They've confused us with someone else, and we were billed for an ad in the paper. Have them reverse the charges, OK?"

Not knowing yet what he was talking about, I pressed him further. "What kind of ad? How much was charged to our credit card?"

"More than a hundred dollars, I'm not sure what the ad is about, but it was entered in the classified section to begin running this weekend," he said.

Oh, no.

I must have looked guilty, because his eyes narrowed. "Joanne, you wouldn't happen to know anything about an ad in the classified section of the *Contra Costa Times*, would you?"

"Ummm, well," I stammered, quickly trying to decipher if he was angry or amused. "I think I might know about an ad, about ummm, well," my eyes were now on the kitchen floor as my toddler squirmed in my arms.

Paul pressed further, "Joanne?"

That was all it took. Just like the kid in the movie *The Goonies*, I spilled my guts all over my blush-tiled floor. "Well, Cutie, you see, I was going to surprise you. I am beginning my own errand-running business." I tried a quirky smile.

"Your own what?" His voice was a little loud. Clearly he didn't understand.

"Errand-running business." I smiled again.

"What's an errand-running business?" His inquisition had now taken priority over being on time for school.

"Well, I was thinking. What business could I do with the kids? Since I'm home most of the day, I thought maybe I could pick up prescriptions for the elderly who don't drive or maybe take people who don't have a car to a doctor's appointment or even pick up groceries for people like caregivers who can't get to the store." I sheepishly smiled again.

There was a long pause. He stared at me as if he was trying to figure me out. Doing his best interpretation of Ricky Ricardo, he smiled. "Lucy. Lucy. Lucy. What am I going to do with you?"

In a matter of minutes, he opened my eyes to how this good idea would be a distraction. Gently, he encouraged me to focus on the best business at hand—the blue-eyed towhead in my arms. Another distraction had been diverted.

I dropped the idea of my cottage business and refocused on the blessed job I'd been called to do—my better choice. But to this day, whenever we are out together and see an advertisement for an errand-running business, my husband gets an elbow to the ribs.

Distraction Support

Since my husband is reigning king of the Land of Focus, he's one of those I've chosen to stand in my inner-hula-hoop of people who hold me accountable. My girlfriend Celia is another. When I run away with a job only half-done and race toward the next bright, shiny thing that calls, these two are the ones who tug and pull, bringing my kite back down again.

I'm attracted to distraction. I'm well aware of my weakness, and it has helped me through the years to have a support system in place to keep distractions to a minimum. I'm inclined to lose focus and not finish what I start, so I share my plans with special people who I know will hold me accountable.

It's not always enjoyable to hear my husband whisper, "Didn't you say you were going to spend time with Samuel tonight?" as I'm happily chatting away on the phone with a girlfriend. Paul likes to flash his distraction-accountability badge whenever possible. I understand now that good things can distract me away from God's best for me.

Dear Lord, forgive me for being distracted. Please give me the focus to achieve every plan you created me for. My heart desires to run off in so many different directions, help me stay put until you tell me it's time to move on. Thank you for the people in my life who gently remind me to finish what I've started. In Jesus' name I pray. Amen.

- Write a list of the five main time stealers in your day.
- Good things can distract from the best things. Are your children taking all of your time each day, leaving no time for your husband?
- Ask two people to be your distraction-accountability partners. Then make a point to share with them what God has put on your to-do list.
- Spend time with the Lord and ask His forgiveness for any covetous thoughts or actions. Thank Him for all He has blessed you with.

Whatever excites the curiosity, scatters the thoughts, disquiets the heart, absorbs the interests or shifts our life focus from the kingdom of God within us to the world around us—that is a distraction; and the world is full of them.

—A. W. Tozer[2]

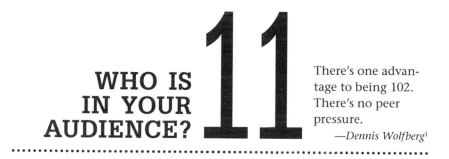

WHO IS IN YOUR AUDIENCE?

There's one advantage to being 102. There's no peer pressure.

—*Dennis Wolfberg*[1]

David, my teenage son, is raising chicks in his bedroom. Yes, I said *in his bedroom*. He's worked out a deal with a friend and will hand them over to be raised in a chicken coop next week. When I sent my oldest daughter, Meghan, a picture of David's chicken room, her text reply to me was, "I don't know where my mom went because the mom I know would never allow that in her right mind!" The truth is, the older I get at parenting, the more tired I've become.

Mothering in my twenties:

"Mom can we have a puppy?"

"No, you already have a dog."

"Can we have a kitten?"

"No. Been there, done that."

"Can we get a bird? We've never had a bird! What about a turtle? Oh, can we collect large hairy bugs?"

"We have most definitely had a bird. Don't you remember when Reagan our parakeet had a stroke? Who was it that found him facedown on the bottom of his cage? Me. And, we gave you a turtle years ago. Fred, your hard-shelled friend, began laying

99

eggs in the aquarium and your father and I had lots of explaining to do with your little brother. I don't mind if you collect bugs, but keep them in the backyard. Grandma almost had a seizure when she slept over and found that praying mantis on her pillow."

Mothering in my forties:

"Mom, can I raise baby chicks in my bedroom?"

"Yes, you can smoke on the back deck."

"I don't smoke, Mom!"

"That's right. I'll go smoke on the back deck."

"You don't smoke either, Mom!"

"What did you ask me, Son?"

"I said, 'Can I raise baby chicks in my bedroom?'"

"Oh, sure you can, Honey."

When I was in my twenties and thirties, I would never have allowed my children to bring chickens into our home. Now that I'm in my forties, a Ma and Pa Kettle lifestyle doesn't seem all that problematic.

Actually, David keeps the chicks in a small cage with a heat lamp, and he keeps it pretty clean. I went into his room yesterday to take a peek at the adorable little yellow and black balls of fluff. Even I had to admit they were pretty cute.

I watched one of the chicks grab a large, colorful piece of hay and proceed to play keep away with his fluffy friends. The other chicks were chasing it and trying to take away the coveted strand. A few of the chicks were just pecking it over and over again. It reminded me of how there were some people during our radical sabbatical who resented the fact we'd made a decision to slow down.

They wouldn't come right out and say it, but they made insincere comments. "Hey, how's that radical sabbatical thing coming along for you guys?" smirking in front of whoever was there. Peck.

"How's Grace doing without playing soccer this season? It must be so hard on her. How can you bear to keep her from something she loves so much?" Peck.

"Wow, I didn't think you guys really had it in you to stick to a whole year of this sabbatical thing. You guys are nuts." Peck.

Paul and I made the decision to live differently for a whole year. We chose not to participate in all of the activities we had become accustomed to being involved in. This made for some uncomfortable moments from time to time. As much as I would love to share how everyone rooted us on to victory, there were plenty of snide comments as well as hushed whispers when I knew we were being talked about, and not in the most glorious of ways.

When you step out of your comfort zone and do something that looks a little bit different, you should be prepared for a bit of opposition that ranges from unkind looks and eye rolls to discouraging comments.

Peer Pressure Parenting

Our feelings were occasionally hurt as we went through our time-out experiment, but not often. The benefits far outweighed the negatives.

Looking back now, I'd do it again. The difference would be that I would do it years sooner.

These things I have spoken to you, that in Me you may have peace. In the world you will have tribulation; but be of good cheer, I have overcome the world. (John 16:33)

Expecting—or even hoping—that our sabbatical would receive the proverbial blessing from everyone was silly. Peer pressure doesn't have the same hold on me that it did in the days of leg warmers, big hair, and acid wash jeans.

Not everyone outgrows peer pressure, though. I've watched parents place their children in sports the children aren't interested in on teams made up primarily of the parents' friends' kids. I consider these parents "members only" people. They are cut from members only cloth. You know, those jackets everyone had to have years ago? These are the people who never outgrew the need to be in the in-crowd. They have no desire to step outside of what everyone else has bought into, regardless of what may be best for their family.

A Great Cloud of Witnesses

God's Word says we are running a race, and in front of others no less! We are being watched by our friends—a great cloud of witnesses. (See Hebrews 11:1-2.) The Lord tells us to lay aside every sin holding us back from enduring our race with joy. For me, this included laying down the sin of pride about looking a little different in front of others.

I'll be the first to admit, when people are watching I stand a little straighter and smile a little wider. A few years ago, Paul and I had a bright idea to take our bikes out for a ride. The weather was beautiful. Though we had never ridden together before, we thought we'd give it a whirl. How hard could it be, right?

It didn't take long before we were winded. I'll never forget how quickly both of us were exhausted and out of breath, wondering out loud how we'd gotten so far from home. Or, better yet, wondering how we were going to make it back alive. At one point, we got off our bikes and hid behind a building, refusing to let the people in passing cars see us out of breath. We stood there hunched over our two-wheelers, laughing like two people who had lost their minds.

Yes, my pride gets in my way from time to time. I might do something or not do something because pride tells me it's what I should or shouldn't do. It's a piece of my heart the Lord continues to work on. Still, my worry about looking silly has diminished over the years. Our radical sabbatical would not have gotten off the ground if I had allowed my concerns about how we looked to friends get in the way.

The longer I meander down the road of less activity, the more I realize that our children are the most important witnesses to our change. While my Heavenly Father was the greatest witness to my deepest parenting desire—to raise them to know and love Him—I also wanted my kids to learn they would survive if they did something outside of what the world deemed ordinary. I want them to discover how extraordinary the unordinary could be. I prayed this would become the foundation for our family's future generations.

Our sabbatical will one day become our kids' bragging rights as adults. They will never be able to say, "I walked to school barefoot in the snow, uphill ten miles—one way." But they will be able to say, "My parents made us stop everything we were doing, and for a whole year they chose to spend time with us."

I'm OK with that.

David's Rooting Section

Some people made derogatory comments about our sabbatical decision, but there were many more in our rooting section. As much as I love being rooted on to victory, I enjoy being the rooter too. When our son sold his pig at the fair to fund his trip to Australia our family got to experience just that.

Australia the pig placed third out of one hundred pigs entered. Pretty good for a first-time novice pig farmer. David named his pig Australia because the money earned from auctioning off his pig was going toward a round-trip ticket to Brisbane, Australia.

In Brisbane they sheer sheep in July, which is our summer and their winter. They call their hired help Jackaroos, and at fifteen years of age, our son was itching to bear that title. Our friend Charlie laughed, "Sure, we'd love to have you, mate. I'd work you harder than your own dad!"

When the day came for the auction, I drove David to the fairgrounds at 5:30 A.M. to feed his pig and get her ready to show. Off in the distance I saw the metal bleachers that would be filled with families like ours before too long. Paul and I had figured out that David's pig needed to sell for $3.82 a pound for him to pay for his trip.

Like a teenager waiting for concert tickets, I staked out my spot front and center in the stands long before the 10 A.M. auction. Hours later, as David walked up to the auctioneer with his prized pig, thirteen of his closest friends and family were sitting right beside Paul and me, whoopin' and hollerin' just as loud as we were.

When the second place pig sold for $3.50 a pound, I was sick to my stomach. What would his *third* place pig go for? *Lord, please show our son favor today. He has worked so hard this year.* The auctioneer's gavel crashed on the table, "Sold for four dollars and twenty-five cents a pound!"

David's rooting section erupted. We stomped our feet, whistled, and cheered. I even cried. For a whole year we had encouraged our son to persevere, to go the distance, not to give up. When he struggled with discouragement, we encouraged him. When he battled disbelief, we told him he could do it. We were his perpetual rooting section.

After our radical sabbatical, I knew who was in our rooting section; specifically, our parents. Grandparents are a key element to a successful rooting section. If you've ever been hurt because they've said, "Slow down. You do too much. These kids will be grown before you know it," don't hold it against them. Their eyes have a much clearer focus on those things with eternal value. No matter how old we are, their desire is to whoop and holler for us too.

Who Is in Your Rooting Section?

Samuel has had a few passions over the course of his young life. One of those passions has been Star Wars. He was at the height of his fascination with Star Wars when he was six years old. At that age it was common to find him pretending to be Luke Skywalker. With his sister and friends in tow, on any given day, they'd have their light sabers attached to their belt loops and run throughout the house and backyard, hunting invisible storm troopers down alien bunny trails. Thanks to Samuel, Luke Skywalker had never been in such daunting situations.

One lazy Saturday, the kids gathered in our bonus room. Apparently, this was the stage our son chose to attempt a move he once saw Luke Skywalker make—a forward flip in the air off of a large steel beam—with light saber in hand. Unfortunately, six-year-olds learn the hard way that movies and reality don't always mesh.

Instead of the beautiful forward light saber flip he saw Luke Skywalker do with such finesse, Samuel's move became an awkward forward flop off an old thread-bare ottoman, giving him just enough air to land on his head with a heavy thud—directly on top of his treasured plastic light saber.

Our son performed this stunt in front of an audience of six- and eight-year-olds. The piercing scream I heard downstairs confirmed his Star Wars exhibition had hit a glitch. My son was accompanied downstairs by his large crowd of witnesses for some first-aid. Samuel learned a few lessons that day. He learned that head wounds bleed a lot and he is no Luke Skywalker.

It reminded me of a Bible study I did with my daughter Meghan and her girlfriend Bridgette when they were in high school. One of the questions asked of the girls stuck with me too: *If you lived your life on a stage, who would be in your audience?*

I can tell you who is often in my audience. From time to time it's my husband, Paul. Oftentimes it's my friends, family, neighbors, and people at church. As a Christian, I should only be concerned with playing in front of an audience of one. Jesus is sitting in the front row waiting to give each of us a standing ovation. He is front and center, rooting us on.

It took a light saber and Samuel's minor head wound to remind me there are no repeat performances in my life. As crazy as our radical sabbatical may have sounded to some, I am grateful for the cheering section that rooted us on to victory.

I believe the Lord is going to ask me some day what I did with the time He gave me. I don't want to tell Him how busy I was performing for an audience of people. I want to live for an audience of one. I want His standing ovation.

Dear Lord, thank you for giving me the courage to live in the world—but not of the world. Give me a heart brave enough to be different. I want my children to learn this lesson while living under our roof. Forgive me for paying too much attention to what everyone else thinks. Thank you for the witnesses you've put in my life, the friends who encourage me to live for you. In my audience, it's your applause I long to hear. In Jesus' name I pray. Amen.

- Is your child in activities he or she wants to be in, or do you find yourself trying to convince your child to participate in activities? How's that working out?
- Do you receive all of your friend time during your child's lessons or practices?
- Who is in the audience you live to please? Is there someone you'd be embarrassed to do a front-flop in front of?
- Make a list of the members of your rooting section.

ENTITLEMENT: THE BULLY ON THE BLOCK

Entitlement children are children who have learned from experience they will get what they want if they demand loud enough or insist long enough.

—*Karen Deerwester*[1]

"Tell me about your relationship with your parents," the counselor asks.

The patient immediately responds with a laundry-list of disappointments and parenting flaws: "My dad never played ball with me. He worked long hours and didn't have time to coach my football team. My mom was an alcoholic and had more boyfriends than I can count."

"Ah, yes, you are a textbook case. Your depression and codependency issues are a direct result of your upbringing." The counselor nods with understanding.

As adults, we understand how parents are the scapegoats for just about everything. And, in some cases, we deserve the blame—abuse, addiction, neglect, ridicule, all disappointing parenting traits that can mold children in twisted ways.

What we don't get to hear enough is this dialogue: "My parents gave me everything. I was taken from activity to activity each day. They bought me name-brand clothes, paid for my first car and my monthly car insurance, and even gave me gas money every week. I grew up thinking I had a right to anything and everything. I believed their financial success was my financial success. When I became an adult, life told me otherwise."

"I'm sorry to tell you this, but you're suffering from a clear case of entitlement," the counselor sadly replies.

Entitlement is when you bestow a privilege—or give a right—to someone. We unknowingly and unceremoniously bestow rights to our children. A right always comes at the expense of someone else, by the way. When we give our children something they have done nothing for or have expended no effort toward, this thing becomes a right, and eventually an entitlement attitude follows. As much as I'd love to sugarcoat an entitlement attitude, I can't. If your children or mine exhibit this trait, it's your fault and mine.

What in the world does entitlement have to do with busyness? Lots.

> **A child with an entitlement attitude accepts no personal responsibility and expects all wants to be filled by you, the parent.**

This attitude is void of one main ingredient—thankfulness. When your children believe they have a right to play soccer, baseball, football, perform in school plays, take dance lessons, or accept every birthday party invitation that finds its way into their backpack, there's nothing to be thankful for, and no one to be thankful to. Thankfulness and entitlement are mutually exclusive.

Thankfulness: The Remedial Lesson

Bending down, a mother hands her daughter a cookie and softly asks, "What do you say?" clenching her chocolate-frosted treasure with dimpled knuckles, she tries to form the words.

Any mommy worth her weight in Pampers will admit two of the very first words taught to her little one are *thank you*. Please and thank you were in three of my children's vocabularies immediately after da-da and ma-ma. Our daughter Grace skipped the original word order and went straight from da-da to "crackaway," which, translated, meant "Cookie, please."

A child is never too young or too old to be taught about thankfulness. The fastest way to remedy an entitlement attitude is to create a home where kids understand some of the sacrifices parents are making and are thankful.

I answered the phone to hear my irate husband give me an earful about our teenage daughter. Her white Toyota Corolla breathed its last alongside the freeway, and we orchestrated ways she could take our second car so she could get to school and work. Coordinating our schedules was a hassle, but like any parents, we love our child and wanted to help her.

Our daughter returned our car to us missing a radio knob, trash strewn about, no gas in the tank, and an odiferous scent of lavender and cheese permeating the air. As my husband drove the vehicle to work, he barked his irritation into the phone. I was instantly reminded of *entitlement.*

When I yelled at Meghan, I mean, when I spoke loudly with Meghan, she shared every excuse imaginable. She didn't have time. She just paid her rent and didn't have money. She didn't mean to. And the all-time entitlement favorite: "I didn't do it on purpose," which children believe is their get-out-of-jail-free card and releases them from any responsibility to right the situation.

On and on she went. Finally, I said, "If you had borrowed your girlfriend's car, would you have returned it to her in the condition you returned ours?"

"No," she answered softly, giving up the fight.

Instead of returning the vehicle in the same or better condition, she felt she had a right to treat our family car as she would her own—or worse! Remember, entitlement shows little or no thankfulness.

Peers Feed an Entitlement Attitude

As our children grow up in a me-first society, what seems to be the norm among their peers can instill a sense of entitlement. Our children seem to think the all-my-friends-have-one argument is a new one.

"Why can't I have a cell phone?" Samuel asked me.

"You're nine years old. Who do you need to call, your stock broker?"

"But all my friends have cell phones. When I gave Gabriel my phone number yesterday, he pulled out his cell and programmed our number into it. I had to write out his number on a scrap of paper." He huffed.

"So because you had to write out your friend's phone number on a piece of paper, Dad and I should buy you a cell phone?"

"Yes," he answered without blinking an eye.

"Well, Honey, if you really want one bad enough you can earn it yourself. But that means you will pay for a cell phone and the monthly service fee too."

"Mom, there's no way I can pay for that. I don't have that kind of money. I'm nine years old!"

"You can do chores around the house and begin earning the money. You could have one in no time." I smiled, calling his bluff.

"Yuck. That's horrible." He looked like he'd eaten a worm.

"Well, then, you don't want one bad enough."

I knew Samuel wasn't interested enough to work at earning his very own cell phone. He felt entitled to one because all his friends had cell phones. Letting children work for something is the oldest and greatest parenting lesson in existence. It teaches them responsibility. So when our teenage son wanted an iPod for Christmas last year, we gave him one with strings attached.

Hard Work—Entitlement's Kryptonite

David's grades weren't what they should have been or could have been. He was barely pulling a 2.5 grade point average and had every excuse in the book as to why he was struggling. This child dazzled me with his impish grin and constant comic relief, and he was trying to win his teachers over with the same performance. Clearly, love makes a difference.

When Christmas rolled around, he had one request—an iPod. A sophomore in high school, he wanted one in the worst way, and he was apparently the only teenager in the western hemisphere that didn't have one. He, too, believed his argument was original.

I want to bless my son. I want to give him everything he desires. I wanted his Christmas morning to be magical and his joy to be off the charts. But, after talking with Paul, we couldn't bring ourselves to give him an iPod. If he couldn't take time to study for a geometry test, why would we give him something more to distract him?

Telling him no was going to be difficult. But I reminded myself that if I'd received all of my requests at fifteen, I would be married to Donny Osmond, driving a purple Pinto, and living in Disneyland. Then I came up with an idea.

On Christmas morning our son was handed a red satin box. He opened it to discover another box and another and another. Opening a ring-sized box he pulled out a slip of paper and read the words aloud: "Merry Christmas, David. This coupon is good for one iPod."

David was thrilled. Looking at us, he reminded me of *Charlie and the Chocolate Factory* when Charlie found the golden ticket. Before he jumped up on our couch and pulled a Tom Cruise on us, I said, "Read the fine print, Son. 'This coupon is redeemable when we receive your 3.0 GPA report card in March. If your grades fall below 3.0 at any time, the iPod is ours.'"

He laughed out loud. "Oh, man, are you kidding me?" He knew we weren't.

In March, David brought home a 3.1 GPA. I immediately went to my husband and shared the good news. Now it was Paul's turn. "Oh, man, are you kidding me? Do you know how much those things cost? Are you sure we promised him this?"

David has taken great care of his iPod. He worked hard for it. This year—his junior year in high school—when he wanted his own cell phone we took him to the local drugstore to pick one out. His weekend soccer referee salary would only allow the pay-as-you-go phone, and as much as I wanted to throw in the money for one with all the bells and whistles, we didn't want to rob him of the success of paying for this on his own.

Life University

Affluence is all around me in the city where I work. It's no surprise to see a teenager driving a BMW to school or to hear of parents handing over weekly spending money to their teen. "Let them have fun," many parents say. "They are only kids once." Yet, these same parents are surprised when little Billy loses his job and wants to move home bringing his wife and kids along.

Parents are robbing their children today. They are taking away opportunities to strengthen their child's resolve, their sense of responsibility, and their hard-work muscles. How will our kids' faith grow if we continue to play God and supply them with all their wants and needs?

I have a friend who has an adult daughter. This young woman has been disrespectful to her parents, especially her mother. Yet the mom continues to help her out financially, to pay her bills and her rent, creating an entitlement monster. This young adult expects and Mom delivers. All the while, this parent is raising a helpless, disrespectful adult woman.

In order for us to stop this kind of behavior in our children, we must make tough decisions. I don't find the words *parent* and *friends* in the same scripture anywhere in the Bible. As the mom, I'm required to discipline my kids. I get the unfun job of teaching them there are consequences to poor behavior and ugly attitudes. If a child has a constant friend in you, then he or she is being raised without a mom.

Sometimes a parent has to be the *bad guy*. If a parent isn't willing to do this, there are going to be big problems down the road. As far as my girlfriend is concerned, she could never dole out consequences and discipline with follow-through, and she kept her husband from doling it out as well. And if a parent can't, life will.

I was working the graveyard shift when the nonemergency line lit up. "Police Department, this is Joanne."

"Hi, I hope you can help me." The woman sounded anxious. "My son parked his car somewhere he probably shouldn't have, and it was towed. He lives about four hours away where he goes to college, and he was told by the local police department that he needs to pay for a tow release *plus* go to the tow yard and pay for the tow *plus* their impound fees. Can they really make him pay for all that?"

"Yes, they can, if he wants his car back," I answered.

"But, my son doesn't have that kind of money. My son is a good boy. He had no idea he would be charged so much. This doesn't seem fair," Mom stammered.

"How old is your son?"

"Nineteen."

"I'm sorry your son parked illegally and he is short on cash. But you might consider trying to let him figure this problem out on his own."

"He called me and was angry I hadn't sent him any money yet. I hate seeing him struggle financially."

"Well, I have a few teens at home myself, and this is what my husband likes to call 'Life University.'"

"I haven't sent him any money *yet*. I'm just asking you for some advice." She acted as if her call was no big deal.

"You're asking me for advice at 2:30 A.M.! You should be in bed sleeping, not trying to figure out ways to solve your adult son's problems. I can promise you this: your son will never park where he's not supposed to again."

"You're probably right. But what should I tell him if he calls and asks me for help with his fines?"

"You want my advice? Next time your son calls, tell him, 'Welcome to Life University. Class is now in session.'"

Kids Will Survive Second Place

When your children's days are filled with shuttling them from guitar lessons to friends' houses to youth group and back home again, why wouldn't they think life is all about them?

That's exactly what you're showing them. If you think your children are immune to this entitlement problem, try telling them you won't be taking them to a few of these places this week because you are exhausted and need a break. Children with entitlement issues are trained to believe they are on equal footing with parents and won't care about your discomfort, only their own.

God has given us the role of parent, and He expects us to carry it out to completion. This includes discipline. If we don't snuff out entitlement now, we'll have arrogant, lazy, self-centered adults on our hands.

When we kept our children out of their favorite activities for a whole year we were saying to them, "Your wants don't come first. Our family comes first." Our children survived second place, and yours will too.

So how do you kill an entitlement attitude? Instill thankfulness and hard work into your children. Thankfulness and hard work are entitlement's kryptonite; works every time.

Dear Lord, I've created children who expect me to fill their every want. Show me ways I can teach them responsibility. Forgive me for making excuses for their poor behavior. When my husband gives out a consequence, seal my mouth shut. Give me creative ways to teach them to be thankful. Help shed the light on ways my children can be encouraged to carry their weight in chores around the house. I desire to help them rather than cripple them. In Jesus' name I pray. Amen.

- When was the last time your child said thank you?
- What responsibilities does your child have around the house?
- Make a list of chores and praise your child when he or she follows through.
- Find ways for your child to work for his or her next "want."
- Put your husband first today and remind your child of the family pecking order!

PART IV

Build

13

ME? PRAY?

To be a Christian without prayer is no more possible than to be alive without breathing.

—Martin Luther[1]

I reached out for the white business card in my husband's hand. Only a name and a phone number graced the front, but I couldn't shake the feeling the Lord was at work here.

"They said they've been driving around our neighborhood and asked if I'd be interested in selling them our van," Paul announced.

"Our Scooby-Doo van? Really? Did they *see* our van out there?"

"I opened it up and let them look inside. The goldfish crackers and McDonald's French fries added a nice touch." He rolled his eyes.

"So they saw the missing bench seat? What about the green van-mucous oozing underneath?"

"Yes and yes. They know about all of it. They told me their sister has a housecleaning business and it would be perfect for her to carry all of her supplies from home to home. They wanted to give me cash right now."

"So why didn't you let them?"

Paul looked surprised. "If I sold it, how would we get around as a family? I don't even know how much the van is worth, Joanne."

"A buck fifty," I shot back.

With four children under the age of ten, two in diapers, our hands were pretty full. Paul had been laid off at his job in San Francisco, and while he awaited the final word that he had been accepted into the California State Bar, providing for all of us was his biggest concern. Each morning at 3:30 A.M. he awoke to throw newspapers. It was two days after Christmas, and we'd been going over our finances when the two strangers knocked on our front door.

"That van is on its last legs," I said.

"Don't you think I know that?" Paul was frustrated. My bad habit of stating the obvious wasn't helping.

"Call them and ask them to come back," I said softly.

"Why?" Paul asked.

"I've been praying for help, and I have a peace about this. I think we should sell them the van." I smiled, reaching out and giving him a hug.

Within minutes, Paul was back outside talking with the new owners of our Scooby-Doo van. They paid us $200 more than its Blue Book value and seemed happy about it. As they drove away I couldn't help smile as our *Got Jesus?* bumper sticker rounded the corner and faded from sight.

Within hours, Paul had purchased a used Chevy Suburban. Later that evening, we piled all of the children in our new car for an evening drive around the neighborhood. We shared what the Lord had done earlier in the day. We reminded them that God knows all our needs and that it's OK to ask for those needs to be met when we pray.

Two days later I recounted the story to my neighbor: "They knocked on our door and said they were scouring our neighborhood for a van they could buy for their sister."

My neighbor interrupted me. "Did you have a For Sale sign in the window?"

"No. That's what makes this so amazing," I continued. "They said their sister has a cleaning company."

"Joanne, we live only a couple of doors down from you, and our van is for sale. We were home all day Sunday, and we've had a For Sale sign on it for weeks."

God had orchestrated it all. He had heard my prayers, every last one of them. It was moments like these that fueled my desire to spend time talking with my Creator. But, as my children grew, so did my busyness, and busyness crowded out prayer every time.

Prayer Is the First Step

I can still remember the afternoon I hit rock bottom, both mentally and physically. Exhausted, I had dropped off one of my children for soccer practice and quickly darted back home to pop dinner into the oven. That done, I ran out of my house and jumped behind the steering wheel to drop my next child off at voice lessons. I silently wondered if any of my neighbors were watching this silliness. My garage door opened and closed like a castle drawbridge in a peewee golf game.

I felt my chest tighten as a crazy vision came to mind. I had become one of those silly circus clowns in a fire truck. Racing back and forth, zipping to and fro, only to once again dart back and forth. This busyness was insanity. I felt just like a clown—absolutely ridiculous. Fighting to hold back tears, I slumped over the steering wheel and laid my forehead against the vinyl ring in surrender. I knew things had to change. But how?

Dear God, please help me was my mumbled midday S.O.S.

Five simple words from the heart of a desperate mom made their way to the throne room of God.

My prayer for help unlocked the door for His will to walk in and play out in my life. Thankfully, the Lord didn't make me wait long for His answer. A crazy-looking decision was on the horizon, and I was finally open for His answer. He knew I would say yes to what He had in store for me. Our radical sabbatical was about to become a reality. Once again, I was reminded that God shouldn't be my last resort. Talking with Him should be my first response.

Prayer: Are You a First Responder?

Emergency service people are called *first responders*. Their first response is to help. Police, fire fighters, and paramedics all race to respond when someone is in need. For many it comes naturally. For most, training is needed to be able to fly into action during an emergency. As a former police officer, my husband was trained to be a first responder.

As a Christian, I have a desire to speak to the Lord about things. But, like a paramedic, there's training necessary before I learn to pray first in a situation. I have to make a conscious decision to do that. His Word is a great reminder.

When I'm going through something difficult, I struggle with taking my cares to God first—before worrying. My first response is to share my anxieties or fears with Paul or have a marathon conversation with my girlfriend.

When I have a weakness, I make a point to teach my children the areas I struggle in, so they can avoid my pitfalls. Things like swimming in deep water, eating more veggies than cookies, keeping my patience while driving—prayer as a first response in every situation. I learned through an emergency experience that they had actually listened to me.

We were just getting onto the freeway, when Paul accelerated to merge with traffic. "Geesh!" I heard him say as a wooden garage door tumbled through the air and landed with a thud, throwing up dust and debris not more than fifty feet in front of us.

We watched in stunned silence as a full-sized pickup truck careened out of control, skidding sideways across three lanes. The driver overcorrected, and the car went airborne. His vehicle cartwheeled off the freeway and over a thirty-foot embankment, landing somewhere below.

As Paul pulled our car over, I silently prayed he would stop our Suburban before the children caught a glimpse of the potential fatality. Quickly, but calmly, he put the car into park and unbuckled his seat belt. "Call 911." Bolting out of the car, he sprinted down the freeway, over the embankment, and out of sight.

As I dialed 911, my hands began to shake; I wasn't familiar with being on this side of an emergency call. As I gave the dispatcher information, I could hear soft voices from the backseat.

My children were praying.

They had been trained to make prayer their first response. I was touched as I listened to them pray for their daddy and the man in the pickup truck.

The looky-loos gathered, pulling their cars onto the shoulder. Some even got out and stood, peering over the edge to view the carnage below. Still, none ran down the steep embankment or attempted to climb over the barbed wire fence.

No one, except my husband.

The driver was alive when Paul got to him, his truck eventually landed upside down on a frontage road below. Partially ejected out the passenger window, he was semi-conscious. Work tools, ladders, and broken glass had been launched and scattered alongside the road, out of the way of oncoming traffic.

Paul thought for sure the driver was dead. We discovered later when the ambulance arrived that his injuries were minor.

I was proud of my husband, but I wasn't surprised. He'd been trained to react this way. My children were proud of their dad too. One moment they were talking with him in the car, and the next they witnessed Clark Kent transform into Superman. First responders are trained to do just that.

What impressed me more than my Superman-spouse was my children's first response. They began to pray, without provocation or direction from me. They'd been trained to bring their cares before the Lord. Someone once shared with me, "Joanne, if all you can do is pray, then that's what you should do." My children lived those words out that day.

But I Don't Have Time to Pray!

I used to believe I was too busy to pray. Not true. Prayer took a backseat in my faith journey for far too long. Making time for it is a discipline I am still learning. At least now I understand I have time for it. How could I honestly believe I didn't have time to talk with God? I made time daily to eat *at least* three meals a day, browse the Internet, and make phone calls to friends who had no power to change the problems I was facing even if they wanted to.

"I don't want to miss my appointment with the King," says evangelist and author Becky Tirabassi.[2] She's one of the Lord's greatest encouragers of prayer and reminds people all over the world we have a part to play in our relationship with our Heavenly Father. She uses the acronym P.A.R.T. to instill this in her audiences.

- Praise: Begin your prayer time with praise. If you don't know how to praise God, read the Psalms. King David can give us all a lesson or two in the praise department. "Praise the LORD, for the LORD is good; sing praises to His name, for it is pleasant" (Psalm 135:3).

- Admit: Confession is good for the soul, as Jesus proved by His own example, "Forgive us our debts, as we forgive our debtors" (Matthew 6:12). Unconfessed sin adds static to our prayer connection. When we confess, He forgives. "If we confess our sins, He is faithful and just to forgive us our sins and to cleanse us from all unrighteousness" (1 John 1:9).

- Request: The Lord wants to hear all of my requests, even the microscopic, seemingly unimportant ones. God promises, all things I ask for in faith, according to His plan and purpose for my life, I will receive. "And whatever things you ask in prayer, believing, you will receive" (Matthew 21:22).

- Thanks: Ending a prayer in thanks to the Lord is a beautiful way to prepare our hearts for the day. When I approach each new twenty-four hours in a posture of gratefulness, the rest of my day runs more smoothly. "Let us come before His presence with thanksgiving; let us shout joyfully to Him with psalms" (Psalm 95:2).

I used to believe prayer was a lesser responsibility for those who didn't have the gift of teaching or couldn't make a great tater tot casserole for the church potluck. Prayer was at the bottom of my to-do list. Those who were labeled prayer warriors, well, I thought it was great for them, but it must be because they weren't gifted for anything else.

The center of power is not to be found in summit meetings or in peace conferences. It is not in Peking or Washington or the United Nations, but rather where a child of God prays in the power of the Holy Spirit for God's will to be done in her life, in her home, and in the world around her.
—Ruth Bell Graham[3]

When I was younger, if I had been given a book to read, I would have voraciously attacked each chapter *except* the one on prayer. After all, prayer was boring, prayer took time, and prayer was only for emergencies, right? I was raised in a church where prayers were memorized and recited and didn't require much reflection on my part.

When I first brought my husband to a service in my childhood church, he was surprised at the lack of emotion, the monotone presentation of those who repeated the same prayer over and over—almost in a chant. Frankly, I wasn't too interested in digging much deeper. As far as I was concerned, prayer was boring, and that was that.

Prayer Changes a Busy Life

Author Lysa TerKeurst gave some wonderful advice to a friend who was suffering from the bondage of busyness.

Cynthia, I want you to write down everything you've done over the past two months. Then take that list and go into your prayer closet and pray. Ask God what items on your list someone else could have done. Yes, I know another person may not have done it as well as you, but that's okay.

Women today are too busy being busy, and much of what we do has no eternal value. Setting priorities and sticking to them requires much time in prayer asking God what He wants you to do and when He wants you to do it.[4]

The busier I get, the more I need to consult the Lord in prayer. How many of you have heard a line like this one? "We only need a teensy-weensy bit of help with the school carnival this year. I'd ask someone else, but no one runs the throw-a-ping-pong-ball-win-a-goldfish-booth as well as you do."

I've learned prayer is not exclusive to the ICU or the Super Bowl. Since our radical sabbatical, I try to consult Him first when ambushed by a school carnival mom. The truth is, I want to say *yes* to everything. I've learned to thank her for thinking of me and tell her I will get back to her. Then I talk to God about it. A friend once shared that when he's ambushed by someone at church, he asks the person, "Have you prayed about *asking* me first?" I loved that.

Prayer is an important part of my day now. I can't imagine how my marriage would suffer if Paul and I spoke only every now and then or just once on Sunday. I'm grateful for a Lord and Savior who not only died for me but who also takes the time to listen whenever I speak to Him.

Have you talked with Him lately? Is He your first step and first response when life gets harried and priorities get skewed? Have you asked Him for help with your captivity of activity? If you haven't, maybe it's time you did.

Dear Lord, what a patient and gracious God you are to wait on me for a moment of my time. I am ashamed that I don't take advantage of quiet moments with you more often. Forgive me when I don't run to you first. I want our relationship to develop in huge ways. Help remind me prayer is the first step. In Jesus' name I pray. Amen.

- Set apart time each day for prayer.
- Pray with your children each night before bed and before they leave for school in the morning. Allow them to overhear your own prayers or see you praying with your husband from time to time.
- Begin a prayer journal. Every couple of months read through it. Your trust in Him will grow as you see how He's been faithful to answer your prayers.
- Find yourself a prayer partner. Some of the sweetest phone calls I've shared have included prayer time with a girlfriend.

EXTREME REST BEGINS WITH SABBATH REST

Rest; the sweet
sauce of labor.
—*Plutarch*[1]

While teaching my Sunday school class a lesson on the Ten Commandments, I asked the children if they knew what a commandment was. Immediately one little boy's hand shot up. "A commandment is what a king gives." What a perfect answer.

God didn't make His Sabbath a gentle suggestion, He made it a command.

**When I started thinking about the Ten Commandments,
I discovered I have a very bad habit of
rating them on a sliding scale.**

Do not murder. Very important!

Honor your father and mother. It's important. Especially if I'm the mother.

Remember the Sabbath and keep it holy. Not too important.

So if my Lord and King commanded me to set apart this day as a day of rest for me and a day of honor for Him, why wasn't I listening?

Being commanded to do something makes my prideful flesh prickle. When I was young, my mom would ask me to fold the laundry. It was easy for me to ignore her kind request. When my dad came home from work and discovered the laundry wasn't folded, he commanded me to finish the task. All of a sudden, the laundry being folded was back on my radar.

I can't begin to count how many times, after my teenagers have said something particularly saucy, I've reminded them, "Honor your mother. It's a commandment, you know!" Before our radical sabbatical I don't recall reminding them once to honor the Sabbath. Our sabbatical gave us time to pay attention to those things we were neglecting, like the Sabbath—just another byproduct of slowing down for a whole year.

Surrendered Rest

Infants will cry and wail when they need rest. We've all watched toddlers go and go and go some more, stopping only when their bodies collapse from exhaustion—falling asleep wherever their tiny bodies have surrendered to their busyness. Our youngest son Samuel is the poster child for this type of surrendered rest.

After celebrating Thanksgiving, our family had just finished saying good-bye to our company. Our children had been given their working orders and the house buzzed: sounds of dishes being cleared, folding chairs being put away, and the noises of the holiday being boxed up permeated every room. Amid the chaos of the busyness, our daughter Grace, who was four years old at the time, announced she couldn't find her two-year-old brother, Samuel. Immediately everything came to an abrupt halt.

After we searched our house top to bottom, he was nowhere to be found. Had our toddler gotten outside and wandered off? Meghan and David left on foot to search the neighborhood. Each second felt like an hour. Paul got in the car to drive around, heading in the opposite direction our two oldest children had gone on foot. As Paul grabbed his car keys, I told him I was going to call the police. "Joanne, try not to panic. Take one more look around the house first."

Paul had been to many of these kinds of calls where a young child had come up missing only to find the child had walked a few houses away. Grace reached up and grabbed my hand as we searched from room to room one last time. Silently praying, I tried very hard to heed my husband's warning and not panic. As I ran up the stairs to the bonus room, I opened the door to our kids' closet, yelling my son's name for the hundredth time, looking again where I'd already looked.

"Mommy, I found him!" Grace shrieked, pointing behind our green couch.

Curled up and tucked against the wall was my little boy. Completely oblivious that his frantic family had sent out a search party and was yelling his name for the past ten minutes. There he lay sleeping. While playing hide-and-seek with Grace, after a long Thanksgiving Day of busyness, his body had surrendered to some much-needed rest as he waited to be found.

It's not much different with me. I have surrendered to my needed rest on my family room couch more times than I can count. An overcommitted life of activity after activity has a way of doing that to me. When I am tired, crankiness usually sets in followed by making the little things in my life the big things in my life. When I'm tired I have been known to start an argument over something as mundane as hanging the toilet paper roll. (*Over* the roll is the correct way to do it, by the way.) Everything becomes distorted and much more stressful. Have you ever felt that way?

Sabbath DNA

God created our bodies with Sabbath DNA.

God placed this spiritual genetic matter within each cell that makes up our miraculous bodies. We can't help it; it's how we're wired. There is no possible way for the human body to keep busy for days or even weeks at a time. Resting is part of our routine maintenance.

We maintain our vehicles with oil changes and new tires, remembering to fill up with gas each week. Rest gives our bodies the renewed ability to move forward toward whatever purpose God created us to fulfill.

I was made in His image. If my God and Creator, the great I Am rested from His labor on the seventh day, how much more do I need rest?

When we decided to take a year-long rest from the busyness of our lives, I realized we hadn't even figured out up to that point how to rest on the one day God gave us to rest in the first place—His Sabbath. Like God's Word promises, we would have been blessed.

> Blessed is the man who does this, and the son of man who lays hold on it; who keeps from defiling the Sabbath, and keeps his hand from doing any evil. (Isaiah 56:2)

Are You Raising Left-Footed Soccer Stars?

Before we took our year-long rest, Sundays had almost become our seventh workday of the week. Many of my friends were running their children to sports activities on Sundays. Not only were they missing out on their day of rest, but they were missing out on time in church together as a family.

Learning how to score a goal with their left foot (which I can do, by the way) is not going to be what gives my children hope, faith, peace, and lasting joy when they are adults. Do you really want to spend future Sabbath Sundays hunting down your grandchildren on soccer fields for a visit?

**What we teach our children to honor now
is very likely what they will honor as adults.**

It may seem as if I'm picking on sports—especially soccer. That's not my intention. It's just that when we drive to church we drive by the soccer field, and it's always a busy place with practices or tournaments being held on Sunday mornings. Soccer is actually one of my favorite sports, and I have enjoyed watching my children play over the years. My fondest high school memories are wrapped around our first place soccer team. I was our league's leading scorer *and* team captain *and* MVP two years in a row, oh, and don't forget most inspirational.

This is usually where my husband softly hums Bruce Springsteen's song, "Glory Days." Truth is, if I were to run down a field today, I'd need to be resuscitated.

For many families, their fondest memories involve sports activities. Who doesn't love to sit under a blanket on the bleachers and cheer for their children? My husband coached football for a few years, and we made great memories. For six months we worked our schedules around four practices a week and a game on Friday nights. It was exhausting, and I fully believe rest and football cannot coexist. But it was lots of fun.

If you're able to have your children involved in sports activities without letting them take the place of home-cooked meals and verbal communication, then you're doing better than we were. It's a slippery slope.

The New Look of the Sabbath at Our House

Our family now approaches Sunday—the Lord's Day—differently. This is the day for rest from the regular grind of life—a time to unplug and disconnect from the world and plug into time with God—by way of restful worship.

We have lunch together as a family or order pizza and invite extended family over for an easy Sunday meal. We turn off the television, and the children can play outside all day, weather permitting.

Maybe your family will choose to honor the Sabbath by turning off video games, iPods, and computers. Encourage your husband to sit back, relax, and take a load off.

Teenage Sabbath Rest

If your kids are young adults, you may be wondering how you can inspire a Sabbath change in them. My husband and I were wondering the very same thing. While watching my kids busy with their iPods one day, I had an idea.

Our two oldest children are teenagers. Something in their genes makes it impossible for them to get through a day without music. One of the changes our family made was to encourage our teens to participate in honoring the Sabbath—set it apart from the rest of the week—by playing only worship music on this day. My husband and I have adopted the same Sabbath music choice. These small changes have made quite a big difference in our home already.

Some Lessons Stick

As I drove Meghan to college this year, I couldn't wait for the two of us to share a six-hour drive in her car. I was looking forward to quality mom-daughter time before we had to say good-bye. I knew she was looking forward to sharing songs on her iPod with me, songs her dad and brother—who were in the car ahead of us—would find much too sappy and girly.

I was touched when she chose worship music for the first hour of our drive. Though it wasn't Sunday, I was grateful my daughter set apart the first hour of our trip for the Lord. I wondered how much of it was for me and how much of it was because she'd learned to love worship music from all of her Sabbath Sundays. I'd like to think it was both.

Sabbath Rest for Parents

The older I get, the more I enjoy a luxurious couple of minutes on my own bed in the middle of the afternoon. I say *on* my bed instead of *in* my bed because I take a nap like a fireman, fully dressed, subconsciously waiting for the next call to bring me to my feet. Before we laid down some nap rules, my husband and I would slip away for a few moments of peace and within minutes we'd hear, "Mom! Dad! *Where are you?"*

Life-and-death questions would then be posed, yelled through our doorjamb. "Where is the mustard?" "Can I have a cookie?" or my personal favorite, "What are you doing in there?" We advised our children to knock only in case of emergency. Soon, sharing their field trip permission slips or letting us know what they wanted for their birthdays in 2038 became emergencies.

Guarding the Sabbath does include protecting some needed time for you and your spouse as well. We decided to school our children on what is and what is not an emergency. We came up with our three-rule plan.

Only three things give our children an open sesame to our bedroom door when we are taking a quick Sabbath siesta:

1. Blood
2. Vomit
3. Fire

Feel free to adopt our family's emergency Sabbath rules or make up rules of your own. Each family is unique, which means there are many ways for families to regulate their very own Sabbath rest.

Guarding the Sabbath

Guarding the Sabbath is one of the hardest things for parents to do. Once we figured out how precious it was to take time together as a family, we wanted to guard our weekly treasure. We had no idea how difficult it would be.

Guarding the Sabbath for us usually begins the moment church service ends. Like clockwork, I feel small hands pulling on my pant leg or hugging me around the waist—their eyes pleading as they whisper loudly, wanting to know if they can invite a friend over.

Some weekends I don't mind at all; actually it's almost easier to rest when they are occupied by the company of their friends.

With a playmate over I don't hear "I'm bored" quite as often. And if they do dare utter the words, we promptly reply, "You're bored because you're boring." Then we recite a laundry list of things they can do for fun. If they take too long to decide, I remind them where the mop and broom are.

Guarding our Sabbath means there are times we need to school our children in the driveway before we leave for church. "No friends over today. After church we're going to have a day with just the six of us." In the case of temporary amnesia and the slight chance they'll forget what we've just told them, we sweetly add the disclaimer, "Ask a friend over today and it will be a very long ride home from church." Guarding the Sabbath can be hard work. But the benefits are well worth it.

Once you have the guarding part down, small changes can be introduced. Here is where honoring the Sabbath can be one small change that can happen for your family.

Are you ready to take a year-long time out? Maybe you desire less busyness and overactivity in your lives, but you aren't ready to commit to something as extreme as a year-long sabbatical from busyness. If you're willing to start with something simple, begin by keeping the Sabbath. Honor the one day each week the Lord has set apart for the sole purpose of worship and rest. In the process you will begin to redeem and regain some quiet time together as a family.

To break the bondage of busyness and begin to see change in your family's lives, start with something that is doable. After all, you eat an elephant one small bite at a time!

Dear Lord, you created Sabbath rest long before you created me. My body needs rest to run well, just as it needs food and water. Help me show you honor on your Sabbath. Help me respect your Sabbath command with joy so my children may learn what a blessed gift you have given us in a Sabbath day. In Jesus' name I pray. Amen.

- Do you rate God's commandments on a sliding scale?
- What change can you make to show your children you honor God's Sabbath commandment?
- Pray for creative ways to honor your weekly Sabbath.
- What stands in the way of a God-honoring Sabbath?
- When you become a grandparent, which of the following do you hope to hear most often?

  "I scored a goal today!"

  or

  "I honored God today!"

PART V

Blessing

FROM DEVOTION TO DEVOTION

Your word is a lamp
to my feet and a
light to my path.
—*Psalm 119:105*

I was not in a happy place. As I walked in the front door, I realized my adorable little Goosey Gander had not finished the chores I had assigned to her. Funny how a mom knows these things instantly. Of course, there had been a few clues. I stumbled over a stray shoe in the entryway, and the lemon-fresh scent of a clean bathroom had not yet replaced last night's noodle casserole fermenting in the kitchen sink.

"Graaace!" I shouted as my cell phone rang. It was Meghan calling from college.

"Hello!" My greeting was a bit sharp.

"Mom?" Meghan sounded concerned.

"Hi, Honey. Sorry about that. I'm irritated with your sister, not you."

"What did she do?" Meghan sounded amused. She had been out of the house for only a year herself, and she thoroughly enjoyed the role of wiser, older, college-aged sister.

Searching the house for my third child as I spoke, "I left her a list of chores to do while I was gone, and it looks like Houdini hasn't done one of them. Grraaace!" I yelled again.

"David and I used to do that to you all the time, Mom. I think you're overreacting."

"I'm what?" Reason isn't well received when I'm in an angry stupor.

"You're overreacting." She repeated herself.

My oldest must be feeling brave when six hundred miles and a cell phone separate us. "I am most definitely *not* overreacting. It's time your little sister learned about keeping her word and following through with her chores. I hope she doesn't have plans for the rest of the day, because Goose is about to act out the role of Cinderella."

Meghan was quiet for a moment. "Mom, I don't want you to get upset when I ask you this."

Great. Here it comes. I hate questions that start this way.

"Have you had your devotion time this morning?"

"What?" I stopped searching for her sister and thought for a moment.

"Did you have time in the Word yet today?" she reworded the question.

It didn't take me long to go through my Saturday morning laundry-list. "No, actually I haven't. It shows, huh?"

"Yep. Sure does." Was she holding back a giggle?

Mom-pride wasn't going to let my little girl get the best of me. "Have *you* had *your* time with the Lord this morning?" I chided.

"Yes, I have." There was a smile in her voice.

It hadn't always been that way. Some mornings I had to hog-tie this child and her I-am-so-bored attitude to sit while I shared a morning devotion with her. A lot had changed since she was a little girl. *Family devotions are yielding their dividends, Lord.* I smiled.

Motherly Devotion

It was the summer of 1978 and I was ten years old. My Aunt Cathy surprised me by showing up to gather my sister and me to go to the box office smash *Grease.* Two hours later, I was singing "Hopelessly Devoted to You" at the top of my lungs and wondering what I could possibly say to convince my parents to send me to Rydell High with Rizzo and Frenchy.

Every woman loves a good romance, and little girls are no exception. When Sandy (Olivia Newton-John) sang about being devoted to her one true love, Danny Zuko (John Travolta), I was hopelessly smitten too. But what did she mean when she sang about *devotion*?

Devote, devoted, devotion—meaning "complete dedication, giving full attention to something—or someone."

How I spend my time sends a clear message to my children about what I'm devoted to.

There was a time when a fly on my windshield would have thought I was most devoted to the role of my kids' social director.

Motherly devotion is marked by dedication, constant attention, and love. A newborn baby doesn't understand *I love you*, but he or she understands Mommy's arms, her tender touch, and her response to a tearful request.

It's important for our children to know they are loved by a God who is more devoted to them than Mom. He has a purpose and a plan for their young lives. There is nothing we can do as parents that is greater than equipping our children with the Word of God. Family devotion time gives us a wonderful opportunity to remind them how God has given many young people starring roles in the Bible to fulfill His plans.

Our radical sabbatical gave us the opportunity to slow down and take time to study God's Word together.

God's Word is a banquet to our souls. And because we crave our Creator's fellowship, we feast upon His Word.

It is written, "Man shall not live by bread alone, but by every word that proceeds from the mouth of God." (Matthew 4:4)

There is no greater lesson we can pass on to future generations than the importance of learning God's Word. If we want to raise our children to know and love the Lord, we will do so by example. When they see us in the Word, they will respect us when we encourage them to do the same.

As much as I'd like to think we will leave our children an inheritance, a property, or a 401K to help them in their old age, the truth is that none of those compare to knowing the love of Christ.

Think about it as the emergency procedures on an airplane. The adult puts on the oxygen mask first, and then puts the child's oxygen mask on the child.

I think some parents shy away from a family devotion because they think they don't know enough. Many Christians seem to be of the opinion that only pastors and churchy-type people can teach God's Word correctly. Wrong!

God works best through humble hearts. There may be times parents will stumble along through the devotion, and those moments can be used as opportunities to share with children that walking with the Lord is a process, a continual journey to get to know Him better.

Watch and Learn from Mothers

Lara, our worship pastor's wife, was an inspiration to me. Because I knew she desired to raise her three children to know and love the Lord, I paid close attention. One of the things I noticed as I got to know her better was that she made a point to have personal time with the Lord in the morning and made sure to do the same with her children.

This was a foreign concept for me. As a baby Christian, I was having a hard enough time finding time for myself, let alone my little ones.

Each morning, before Lara sent her children off to school, she gathered them around the kitchen table. Sometimes she read a story to them from the Bible, other times the children took turns reading a verse, some days she shared what God had been showing her.

She began the day with the Word and a simple prayer before she launched them out into the world. She was doing more than packing their lunches and stuffing their backpacks with schoolbooks. She was arming them for battle.

Therefore take up the whole armor of God, that you may be able to withstand in the evil day, and having done all, to stand. (Ephesians 6:13)

I knew this was something I wanted to do with my own children, so I went out and purchased a children's devotion book, and we began.

Some days it was wonderful; other days, it was a blessed event. But there were days when the children were arguing or in a rush, or I was in a mood, and the time was not as pleasant.

Never underestimate how the enemy will try and sabotage precious time together in His Word. Persevere and continue on.

Be Devoted to Change

Of course, it wasn't long before I wanted my husband to be part of this devotion time with the children. Since he is self-employed, he was home most mornings. *Why isn't he leading our family devotion? He is the spiritual head of our home. He should be leading, not me,* I stewed. Imagine my irritation and anger when he didn't want to participate!

A little tip for moms who want to make a change and begin a family devotion time in their homes: focus on *your* change, not your husband's. Don't expect your husband—or your children for that matter—to be in the same spot on their faith journeys that you are in yours.

Years later, my husband did begin to lead our devotion time. I'm ashamed to admit how many heated arguments we had over this very thing. There is nothing uglier than a nag, and I'm sorry to say I was a world-class, Olympian nagger for a while.

> Better to live on a corner of the roof than share a house with a quarrelsome wife. (Proverbs 25:24 NIV)

Devotion Ideas

If you have little ones, establishing a devotion time will be a breeze. Young children love to sit on Mommy's lap and hear a story and say their prayers.

Teenagers could be more of a challenge. I suggest you begin in Proverbs.

The thirty-one proverbs were written by King Solomon, son of King David and Bathsheba. Solomon was considered to be the wisest man in the Bible. He asked for wisdom from the Lord, and as is the way of our loving Father, He gave it abundantly.

Teens are often lacking in the wisdom department. I know this is true, because I was once a teenager myself. So Proverbs would be a great place to start.

If your teenager is accustomed to a morning devotion time, alone or with you, I suggest stretching his or her comfort zone a bit. How about letting your teen lead the family devotion?

When it was clear our two older children, ages fourteen and seventeen at the time, were beginning to feel they were too old for the daily Bible stories we were reading with the younger two, I invited them to host devotions for all of us. It was amazing. Each had a teaching style and brought laughter to our time together. And I can tell you that it does a mother's heart good to hear an almost-grown child share what he or she knows to be true about God.

Here are a few ways I've learned to make family devotions fun and nag-free.

- Have a set time to gather together. Maybe your mornings are the best time for your family; set an alarm to get up a little bit earlier if need be. The devotion doesn't need to be long and drawn-out.

- Make it fun. Smile and laugh with your children; resist the urge to be pompous or to lecture.

- Allow your children to lead the family devotion from time to time. As they learn to read, let them take turns reading the Bible verse or the story of the day. Teenagers can lead family devotion on the weekends. It is encouraging and satisfying to watch them grow in their knowledge and understanding.

- You can read from a daily devotional book or talk about what they learned at Sunday school or what you learned in a Bible study.

- It is not important where or how you start, only that you start.

Start Today

It's never too late to begin. Sure, it's easier to begin when children are younger. Preteens and teenagers have a difficult time with change and may attempt to buck the new system. Hold those reins tightly, Mom. As much as they protest, these will be the moments they remember. They will be touched by the fact that you are spending time with them.

Looking back, I don't think it was a coincidence that our radical sabbatical was birthed on New Year's Eve. God knew our family's tradition is to share a special New Year's Day devotion together. He allowed our family devotion time to set the stage where Paul and I would announce the new changes we were going to be making as a family.

As long as you are breathing, there is time to make essential changes. A family devotion is a wonderful way to start. Teach your children from devotion to devotion to Him.

Dear Lord, help me make time in the day to teach your Word to my little ones. Let me be a good example and wholly devoted to you. Let my children see the value of a daily devotion. Help my children grow from devotion to devotion—to you. In Jesus' name I pray. Amen.

- Look back over your day. What would your family say you have been most devoted to today?
- Set apart a little time to be in God's Word today. Ask the Lord to reignite your devotion to Him.
- Ask your children to share their favorite Bible stories.
- Have you begun a regular family devotion time with your children? If not, begin today!

SLAYING YOUR MEDIA DRAGONS

16

For all our constant connectivity, our electronic devices often keep us apart.
—*Elizabeth Bernstein*[1]

Exceedingly abundantly more is God's modus operandi. When we slowed down for a year, I should have known the Lord was going to teach us exceedingly abundantly more than we had bargained for. Less chaos in our schedules meant more peace. When the fog of busyness began to lift, we had a clear view of other areas that were in need of a tune-up. One of those areas was technology.

Flipping through the pages of *Good Housekeeping*, I came across an article that, among other things, stated that heavy media users reported lower grades and happiness levels. The article also quoted statistics from a Kaiser Family Foundation Study, "Generation M2: Media in the Lives of 8- to 18-Year-Olds" <www.kff.org/entmedia/> accessed in January 2010:[2]

- Kids spend more than seven and a half hours with media— TV, iPods, and the Web, *plus* another two hours on their cell phones, per day.

- Seventy-one percent of all eight- to eighteen-year-olds have their own television in their rooms.
- Eight- to eighteen-year-olds spend only thirty-eight minutes a day reading from a book.

Are you concerned yet? As our own children became teenagers, bloody battles over Facebook, video games, and iPods were waged. We strategized our plan of attack and put the cell phone and television first in our crosshairs.

My husband and I love slaying media dragons in our home. The cell phone is one of the easiest to kill in our opinion. We haven't fallen victim to the electronic feeding frenzy of this generation, because we know we parents hold all the cards.

Our teenager asked one day, "Mom, can I get a cell phone?"

While she rambled off a list of reasons and made a strong case, I had a flashback.

"But, Mom, I neeeed a pager," I whined.

"You need one, huh?" Mom looked up at me. Cutting carrots for her pot roast no longer held her full attention.

"Yes, I need one. Everyone has a pager. I'm the only teenager in the state of California that doesn't have a pager. It's embarrassing." I sighed and brushed aside my big 80s hair for emphasis.

"Who do you think you are? A heart surgeon? Does General Hospital need to page you for transplant surgery?"

"No," I huffed.

"Then you don't need a pager. You want one. A need is not a want," she reminded me, and went back to preparing dinner.

Paul and I knew cell phones weren't going away. "A teen's greatest time stealer is the cell phone," my friend reminded me. Did this mean I'd have to fight this jingling pest from strong-arming my child's full attention? We decided to discourage it for as long as possible.

Once our children were driving and had their own part-time-job income, we discussed this electronic nuisance once again. This time we were armed with a few family rules.

- Your Dime Not Ours: If our teenager wants a cell phone, he or she must purchase it with his or her own money. This includes the monthly service fee—which means for us that cell phones don't come on the scene until said teenager has a part-time job and a 3.0 grade point average.
- Seen but Not Heard: It's incredibly rude for a cell phone to bully its way into a family moment with a chirp, whistle, or jingle. When our teen comes home from school the cell phone is put away in his or her purse or bedroom. If it's not, it gets a day or two time out—in *my* purse or bedroom.
- Operating Hours: Did you know cell phones are nocturnal? They come alive when everyone goes to bed. Young adults are electronic wizards, yet they can't find an off button to save their lives. Cell phones in our home have a reasonable bed time.
- Your Cell Phone Is My Cell Phone: If our child has a problem controlling his or her calls or texting habits, we have no problem taking the phone. It's a great disciplinary tool. If our child reminds us, "You can't take my phone. I bought it and pay for it myself!" My husband reminds him or her, "Yes, and you have that great monthly service fee because you're on *our family plan*. Go ahead; get a plan of your own. Oh, that's right; you have to be eighteen years old to sign up for a cell phone plan."

Reality is a cold bucket of water on a teenage cell-phone fire.

Television: My Drug of Choice

As the matriarch of our home it wasn't long before I realized I was plugged in—*a lot*! When I looked around, it seemed we had a seventh member of the family—our television set. When I stopped to think about it, there were days I gave more of my undivided attention to the television than to my four children combined. It was my daily drug of choice, taking me to faraway places, allowing me to peek inside homes I prayed were more dysfunctional than ours, and it taught me more about great white sharks than I cared to admit. Yes, I loved my television set. I couldn't imagine living without it.

Unfortunately, what was originally created to add a small slice of entertainment quickly became the media bully on the block. With my full consent, I allowed this fire-spitting dragon to take center stage in our home and become the biggest time stealer in our lives.

"Like the sorcerer of old, the television casts its magic spell, freezing speech and action and turning the living into silent statues," says psychologist Uri Bronfenbrenner. "The primary danger of the television screen lies not so much in the behavior it produces as the behavior it prevents—the talks, the games, the family festivities and arguments through which much of the child's learning takes place and his character is formed."[3]

Here are some other interesting statistics:

- Families communicate an average of forty percent less when the television is on.[4]
- Forty-five percent of all eight- to eighteen-year-olds live in a home where television is on all day, regardless of whether anyone is watching.[5]
- Sixty-four percent of all American households watch television while eating dinner.[6]

Television Rehab

"Paul, if I rearrange the furniture, when can you reconnect the cable?"

"Not until late next week. I'm swamped right now," he replied as he headed into his office to make some calls.

I wasn't really concerned about it. Surely we could last a few days, right? I was, though, a little worried about how Paula Deen was going to take the news.

A few weeks later, I was in the kitchen when Paul came up and told me he had time to reconnect the cable now. As he walked into the garage to gather his tools, David, age fourteen, overheard our conversation

"Mom, is Dad going to hook up the TV right now?"

"He sure is." I smiled, eagerly anticipating my tearful homecoming reunion with Paula.

"Why?"

"What do you mean, *why?*" I was shocked. My less-than-HGTV-approved kitchen came back into view. I looked at him, wondering if I'd actually heard him right.

"It's just that things have been so nice and quiet around here lately. Having the TV off has been, I don't know, *nice,*" he said softly as he walked out of the kitchen.

Was this really happening? My teenage son, who loved Animal Planet and the Discovery Channel, was making an uncomfortable plea, putting together words uncommon to the average teenager. *Having the TV off has been nice.* What was going on here? When had he joined my husband's team? David was now on the side of peace in the home, casting his vote to throw our television off the island.

I was at a crossroads. The way I figured, I had two choices: I could work fast to convince both my son and my husband that during our most recent television fast we'd learned how to curb our viewing time, or I could step into uncharted high-definition waters and do something a little radical.

Paul came in from the garage carrying his tools. I shared with him what our son had just said. He was surprised too. I looked at him and said, "OK, you win. I think we should keep the TV off for now. If our teenage son is doing OK without it, I could try and go a little bit longer too."

Content Desensitized

Celebrating our anniversary at a bed and breakfast getaway, for the first time ever, we requested a room with a television. Dropping our bags, we raced for the holy grail of our room—the remote. Overjoyed, like giddy five-year-olds on Christmas morning, we laughed as we struggled in hand-to-hand combat.

Since both of us were starving for some broadcasting entertainment, we voraciously channel-surfed, but found little worthy of our time.

When we attempted to watch a weekly series, we were soon privy to a sex scene that made even our middle-aged cheeks blush. Changing the channel, we watched women in string bikinis selling everything from hamburgers to skill saws. Was there a commercial that didn't use sex as its selling gimmick? We had a hard time finding one. When did things like toe fungus and sensitive feminine products become open-season for a daytime advertisement? What had happened to television in the few months we had stopped watching? We racked our brains and finally figured it out:

Absolutely nothing.

Television hadn't changed in two months. We had. We'd been aware of the time-stealing aspect of the television, but we realized we'd become desensitized to the sex-selling schemes and commercials about dryness and itching. Through the years, it had become white noise. It got us to thinking.

Before unplugging, we weren't paying attention to everything that blared into our home each time we hit the on button. But what if our kids were? I silently thanked God for a husband who had stood his ground when I attempted to convince him what a great idea it would be for each kid to have a personal television in his or her bedroom. What in the wide-world-of-sports had I been thinking?

We turned off the television and recommitted to continue our television fast as long as we could. We were grateful our teenage son wasn't left home to watch whatever he wanted. With pornography now only a click away on our laptops, our sons were not going to have those freedoms either.

We knew we couldn't control everything our kids watched or heard, but we were taking a stand in our own home to create a safe place to raise our children in a way that was God-honoring. We didn't want them to be confused by voices in a box telling them things like casual sex or selfishness was the norm.

Thankfully, in this day and age, curbing our television lust is possible. We enjoy our weekly family movie night together, popping popcorn and watching a DVD. And, from time to time, Paul and I watch a favorite show on our laptop. I really don't miss it.

What About the Kids?

We've been a television-free family for almost three years now. You're probably wondering how the kids are holding up. Meghan was the only one who begged us to hook it back up. When she moved out, she ended her television fast. Her words encouraged me, "Mom, I'm so grateful you and Dad kept us from watching all the junk on TV. There's so much out there I wouldn't want Grace and Samuel to watch—David either."

Academically, our children seem to be thriving. Meghan is a junior in college, taking twenty-four units this semester; she also works twenty-five hours a week at a part-time job. David went from getting Gs (we called them Gs because they were even lower than Fs!) in grammar school and is now pulling a 3.5 GPA as a junior in high school. Grace is now twelve years old and in junior high. She was in the gifted program at her grammar school and loves math and time with her girlfriends. Samuel is now in the fourth grade and is also in the gifted program. Last year, when he was nine years old, he set a record by reading 10,000 pages in a quarter.

How much of this is genetic and how much of it is influenced behavior? I'm not sure. Could good grades be due to time freed up from the television and excess media use? I like to think so.

I don't want to give the appearance that I'm just picking on cell phones and television. I understand there are other media tools of influence and distraction in homes. Television just happened to be our Goliath. Limitations on all things techy can give you more time as a family—Facebook, texting, and Twitter. For now, we are still working on slaying the video game-iPod-laptop giants. Give us time.

Set Apart Electronics

"Meghan, I just bought a new laptop, and I know you need one for college. Would you like my old one?" Paul made the offer in a phone call.

"Yes, please, I'll be right over!" she shouted into the phone. Within minutes she was in Paul's office for him to explain the cords and doodads. As he passed his laptop from his hands to hers, he looked her in the eyes, "Keep it holy, Meghan."

Meghan recently shared with me how the words from her father stayed with her. "You know, Mom, when Dad handed his laptop to me and told me that, his words stuck with me. I'll never forget it. And you know what? To this day, I haven't watched anything on it that would disappoint him."

What a charge to keep. It made me ask myself, *Do I keep every-thing from my cell phone conversations to television time to my laptop holy and set apart?*

If the Lord were to pull up a chair and spend some media time with me, would He be disappointed?

Doing something out of the ordinary like saying no to cell phones during family time or unplugging the television may look radical to the world, but that's OK, because we weren't given our gift of life to please the world. We unplugged our television one year after finishing our year-long time out. We were getting used to taking radical sabbaticals.

Slaying media dragons is a constant battle. But Paul and I are up for the challenge. We have been given only so much time to raise our four God-given treasures. We want to make our time count in a way that will mark our children's lives by their relationships with us and one another, not silly ringtones or season finales. Marcia Brady and Laura Ingalls were the greatest influence in my young world, but when it comes to our children, we're choosing to be the greatest influence in theirs.

Dear Lord, help me guard my children from electronic distractions. Remind me that it's OK to say no more often. Open my eyes to the things I watch on television that could send mixed messages to my children. My heart's desire is to raise kids who love you and honor you. Give me the strength to go on a cell phone, computer, or television fast of my own and the courage to bring my family along for the ride. In Jesus' name I pray. Amen.

- Turn off the television and hand your child a book.
- Create cell phone, iPod, and video game rules for your family.
- Unplug on Sundays and give your electronics a Sabbath rest.
- What media dragon terrorizes your family most? Slay it!

A NEW THING

17

God is in the "new
thing" business.
—Joanne Kraft

"Behold, I make all things new" (Revelation 21:5). Six tiny words of scripture that pack a supernatural punch! This scripture promise may be the one that is dearest to my heart. When we began our sabbatical journey, I had no idea the lessons He would teach me about *new things*; lessons that included letting go of past mistakes so they could no longer hold me back. Only after I became a Christian at the ripe old age of twenty-nine did my life become a testimony of their truth.

Driving home from work, I felt the deepest despair I have ever known. My life was a jumbled mess of rebellion and broken commitments. I can still remember peering over the edge of a two-lane canyon road, high atop a hill. One hard right turn of my steering wheel and all of my pain would be over.

Thankfully, I never made good with my painful desires. The hard right turn I did make was into the open embrace of Jesus Christ. The choice was easy. He promised to make all things new for me. Who wouldn't want that kind of deal? *Why doesn't everyone say yes to Jesus?* I often wonder. I'm not sure I will ever understand it.

He wooed me to himself and was living water to my parched soul. Everywhere I turned He was there. He came to me through my supervisor at work, a former missionary from Ireland who shared the resurrection story with me as I worked at an old police radio console in the middle of the night. He was the prayers of my dad and his umpteenth attempt to get me to read the Bible or listen to sermons on tape. He was the encouragement of my coworker Celia, dragging me along with her to church after working a graveyard shift together.

Ever so gently, He began to make all things new in my life. It was during this time that I accepted a marriage proposal from a police officer I worked with. He was everything I could ever imagine wanting in a man. Not only was he brilliant, funny, and handsome, but his kind and gentle heart was salve to my own—still cut and bleeding. He was my knight in shining armor, rescuing the poor damsel in distress. At least, that's probably how it looked to those who refused to give God credit.

On a clear fall day in November we were married. Together there wasn't anything we couldn't conquer. In front of a handful of guests I vowed to love the man I believe the Lord created me for. God again was working to make all things new.

I soon discovered God wouldn't ask me to let go of something without giving back in blessings. After my mother died, my father remarried. We were hurt that he remarried so soon. But I couldn't dislike my stepmother, Linda, if I tried. And sadly, I tried. A godly woman and prayer warrior who loves my father and loves me and my children as her own, she was the beauty from the ashes of my mother's death. God, once again, was making all things new.

Years before I signed my first book contract, I felt the Lord doing another new thing in me. He was giving me the desire to write for Him. I had begun praying that if it was His will He would allow me to share my love for Him through my writing.

Brushing my teeth one evening, I yelled back at my husband who was reading in bed.

"Paul, I'm going to write a book one day."

Getting no answer, I yelled through my garbled mouthful of toothpaste and spit for emphasis, just in case he hadn't heard me.

"Paul. Did you hear me? I said I'm going to write a book one day. Do you believe me?"

"Yes, I believe you," he yelled back. "You'll do anything to keep from cleaning house."

New things are Jesus' specialty. No matter what our age or education, our weaknesses or our fears, He makes us new creations.

Therefore, if anyone is in Christ, he is a new creation; old things have passed away; behold, all things have become new. (2 Corinthians 5:17)

God is so serious about making all things new that He didn't like for me to spend too much time looking back at former things. He didn't want me to dwell on the past; He wanted me to focus on the new things He was doing.

Do not remember the former things, nor consider the things of old. Behold, I will do a new thing, now it shall spring forth; shall you not know it? I will even make a road in the wilderness and rivers in the desert. (Isaiah 43:18-19)

His Word says the old has gone. *Look over here! See what I'm up to! I'm doing something new. Forget the former hurts and pain.* The past fogs up our mirror so we can no longer see the new things He is busy doing. I learned to be very careful not to spend too much time traveling down memory lane.

Memory Lane

My husband is my reluctant passenger whenever we travel down memory lane. Once I put on my turn signal and head toward recollection road his body stiffens, and his eyes roll back in his head in silent protest. It's at this moment I commit a felony—a marriage felony. I become his kidnapper and he becomes my unwilling hostage. Any questions I ask him like, "Paul, do you remember that time . . . ?" or "Paul, have you ever . . . ?" instantly transforms his countenance. I recently was able to share my husband's pain. While pursuing a part-time job at a local police department I experienced a polygraph test.

It probably isn't fair to compare the stress of a polygraph test with taking a quick trip into the past. But I believe the similarities are striking. Like my husband, as soon as the polygraph technician began asking me questions, I immediately tensed up. She quizzed in rapid fire, "Have you ever lied to your supervisor? Have you done anything in the past ten years you are ashamed of? As far back as you can remember, have you stolen something from your employer, even as a teenager?"

I silently thought, *As far back as I can remember? Seriously? A teenager? Are we going back that far?* My mind was trying to work the numbers to figure out if my infractions were still admissible in court. I was thinking of answers even before the technician could ask the questions.

I nervously wondered, *What's the statute of limitations on stolen peanut butter cups?* At one point I almost blurted out loud, "I never inhaled!" As my mind raced I became anxious, *Should I call my attorney for legal representation?* As the questions continued, just like my husband's, my body stiffened and my eyes rolled back in my head.

It didn't help that I was sitting in a chair that was monitoring my breathing, my sweat production, and my heart rate. Like an electric chair, but without the deadly result. Instead, I was the one who wanted to die and be relieved of this man-made time-machine. Some of the questions brought back memories I was not excited to answer. While other questions brought back memories I was not proud of and some that are actually quite shameful.

As I was driving home from the polygraph I felt miserable. Like any woman who had just thrown up every bad memory, I began my trek home by drowning my sorrows in a double cheeseburger and triple-thick milkshake. My past was laced with sins I had not thought of in a long time.

With my mouth stuffed full of French fries, the Lord reminded me of the story in Genesis when the angels grabbed Lot and his wife and daughters by the hand and pulled them to safety from the destruction soon to befall Sodom and Gomorrah.

As soon as they had brought them out, one of them said, "Flee for your lives! Don't look back, and don't stop anywhere in the plain! Flee to the mountains or you will be swept away!" (Genesis 19:17 NIV).

Not only were they to flee for their lives, they were commanded to not look back. They weren't to saunter, stroll, or even loiter in the past. Good advice for me too. The Lord gave this command to protect me from feeling miserable. Well, of course, I was feeling miserable. I had just spent three painfully long hours meandering down the road of my sinful past. God's Word says I am not to look back there and never stop anywhere along the sinful road of remembrance.

The enemy loved every bit of my polygraph test. No doubt he would have loved to have kept me back there in my Sodom and Gomorrah days. I was struggling to not believe this was who I truly was. Thankfully, I had learned from a dear friend that whenever I felt myself believing lies I was to use God's Word as a sword of truth to slice and dice wrong thinking.

God's Word is supernatural and more powerful than any deep-breathing exercises or 800 milligram Ibuprofen tablet to take away the pain and shame of my past. Only after washing my mind in His Word did I have peace. God's peace is a by-product of His gift of grace. Undeserving, unmerited favor is the supernatural soap that washed me clean, from the inside out.

God created me—and you—with an amazing brain. It not only functions as a bad memory retriever but can also bring back to mind many beautiful memories as well. There is nothing wrong with looking back at baby photos of my children or love letters from my husband. God has gifted me with the ability to look in life's rearview mirror from time to time to see all of the special moments I've been gifted with. The reality is, while driving forward on Memory Lane, I can only look in my rearview mirror for a moment. If I keep my eyes on the past I won't be able to go forward very well and might eventually crash.

Jesus reminds us in the gospel of Luke to remember Lot's wife. He wants me to be cautious, because looking back keeps me from moving forward and drawing closer to Him. That is why this is called a Christian *walk*, not a Christian *stand* or a Christian *stop*. Christianity is a moment-by-moment process. As I continue through this supernatural journey, I'm praying I'll take steps forward as I grow and mature.

As a blessed child of our King, He promises to work everything out for the good for those who love Him. I'm thankful for my polygraph test. What began as a nauseating recollection of the miry muck of my sinful past became a great reminder to me of God's grace, mercy, and forgiveness.[1]

Watch and See

- "Then He who sat on the throne said, 'Behold, I make all things new.' And He said to me, 'Write, for these words are true and faithful'" (Revelation 21:5).

- "Therefore, if anyone is in Christ, he is a new creation; old things have passed away; behold, all things have become new" (2 Corinthians 5:17).

- "Do not remember the former things, nor consider the things of old. Behold, I will do a new thing, now it shall spring forth; shall you not know it? I will even make a road in the wilderness and rivers in the desert" (Isaiah 43:18-19).

While preparing to speak at a women's conference, these three verses kept coming up. *Lord, do you want me to share about "new things" with the ladies?* Over and over the verses kept coming to my mind. It was settled. I would share how He can make all things new in our lives. But as I began to dig deeper into each verse, the word "behold" came into view.

In the New Testament, the Greek word for *behold* is *idou,* which means "to watch and see; to be in the presence, or in attendance." It is an action verb, telling us God is actively working at this very moment to make something new in our lives.

What I found even more breathtaking was He asks each one of us to be present while He works. Can you believe that? Little ol' you and me, in the presence of the Lord as He creates and forms, builds and raises, a thing of beauty from my life. God knew how I needed Him to create a new thing from the old busyness I was burdened with.

I imagined a classroom with the Lord standing at the front of the room taking attendance.

"Jennifer?"

"Here."

"Amy?"

"Here."

"George?"

"Here."

"Tanya?"

"Here."

"Wonderful. You are all here." The Lord smiles. "Now I can begin. I've asked you to be present today and experience my glorious work." Their faces look hesitant. You see, each person walked into the room earlier, dumping tattered hurts and shameful heartaches into His arms, holding back nothing.

Jesus pauses. Gathering up every last tattered and torn, shameful and ugly thing they'd deposited earlier, He leans toward them just a bit and whispers in a warm voice heard in the very core of their beings, "Now watch and see what I can do."

Jesus is the author and perfecter of our lives. What is holding you back from seeing the *new things* He is doing for you? What old things are clouding your vision? Is your sight blurred by the bondage of busyness or the captivity of activity? Try to remember what His Word says: He makes all things new. He is doing a new thing. You are a new creation. And through it all, He prefaces His Word with one, *Behold*.

He is waving His hands and yelling in your direction. "Look over here, pay attention, fix your eyes on me, and watch what I can do."

Dear Lord, forgive me for holding on to the past. Keep me from driving the wrong way down Memory Lane. Help me keep my eyes ahead, focused on you. New things frighten me. Wrap your arms around me when I hesitate. I desire to have a front-row seat while you make all things new in my life. In Jesus' name I pray. Amen.

- What *old things* are tripping you up? Pray and ask God for help.
- What three *new things* have you always wanted to do but have never had the time? Do one this week. No excuses.
- Do you loiter on Memory Lane? Move along before God hands you a ticket.
- Go out for coffee with a friend and share your testimony. Explain the areas where He has made all things new for you.

REDEEMING THE TIME

18

Redeem thy mis-
spent time that's
past, and live this
day as if thy last!

—*Thomas Ken*[1]

Sitting in Mrs. Bagai's second grade class, I raised my hand to ask the date, "Today is March 2, 1976," she answered. Leaning down she whispered, "The only March 2, 1976, in your lifetime." Her eyes smiled behind her large-rimmed glasses. Her words stopped my number two pencil midsentence. It was my very first thought about the gift of time.

God's Word is filled with lessons on time. The word *time* is weaved through the Bible and found in more than six hundred scriptures. So why did God inspire the apostle Paul to write about redeeming time?

Therefore be careful how you walk, not as unwise men but as wise, making the most of your time, because the days are evil. (Ephesians 5:15-16 NASB)

Walk in wisdom toward those who are outside, redeeming the time. Let your speech always be with grace, seasoned with salt, that you may know how you ought to answer each one. (Colossians 4:5-6)

The Lord warned us to be careful with our time. He considers it a wise thing when I use time deliberately, with precision and purpose—not wasting it foolishly. Only then will I use it to the best of my ability, taking advantage of every opportunity He has purposed for my life—redeeming the time.

Regain Time

Author Elizabeth George, speaking at a women's conference, asked, "If your children needed to leave you an urgent note, where would they put it?"

I would love to think my children would stick my note on the cover of my Bible or on any one of their foreheads. But sadly, my note wouldn't be in any of those places. My son Samuel, unknowingly, showed me just where he would place mine.

He was thrilled when he won the prize for a class competition. A packet of morning glory seeds was the coveted plunder. Knowing how much I love flowers, he carried the seed packet home for me in his backpack.

My precious little boy wanted to surprise me and thought long and hard about where he could put them. Impatient after his walk home from school, he knew just where I'd discover them immediately.

"Mom, have you been on your computer yet today?" he asked.

"No, Honey, I haven't." My laptop was where I'd last left it, by the side of my bed.

"Mom, I think you need to open it up." Samuel smiled, barely able to contain himself.

Walking over, I opened my shiny red laptop to discover the treasure inside. There on my keyboard was his prized package of flower seeds—his gift to me.

I hugged him tight. "Samuel, I love morning glories! I can't wait to plant them. And I know just where I can find a helper." He grinned from ear to ear and nodded enthusiastically. All the while my heart was hurting.

Hugging my son, Elizabeth George's words haunted me. *Where would your child leave a note for you, if they wanted to make sure you would get it? Would it be by your telephone or your computer? How about on your TV? Or is it possible they would leave your note on your Bible?*

Memories flooded back. As a child, I knew exactly where I would have left my note for my mother—on her telephone. She was on the phone constantly, making it very clear to my little girl heart that her friends came first. What I would have given to have her hang up the phone and spend an afternoon talking with me.

My family shouldn't take every waking moment of my time, but they should know they rank above my laptop. I want to discover my next packet of morning glory seeds pinned gently to the heart of my husband and children.

I have only been given so much time. I can't manufacture any more. But I can survey how I'm using it. When I stop and take account of how I'm investing it, I regain a surplus of time for the future. The busyness we had been experiencing needed to be redeemed. I had to remind myself there was still time to change the location of my note. And as long as I'm on this side of heaven, God has the power to help me redeem my time.

Your Spiritual Alarm Clock

Samuel wears two watches. Night and day, he wears them both. One is waterproof, which means it keeps him company in the shower too. He is our family town crier, announcing the time in two-minute increments as we try to dash out the door in the morning.

"It's seven-thirty, Mom. I really want to be at school early." He stands at our front door—the hump of his backpack protruding like a miniature but extremely bossy Hunchback of Notre Dame.

Buying myself a couple more minutes I yell questions from the other side of the house, hoping to distract his obsession with time. "Did you brush and floss your teeth? Have you made your bed? Did you make your lunch?"

"Yes. Yes. And Yes. C'mon, Maaawwwwwm, I want to play on the playground for a few minutes." He loudly sighs. "It's seven-thirty-two, Mom!"

God's Word says we were created with eternity in our hearts. He purposed time just for us. Deep inside of us, He placed a time-sensitive spiritual alarm clock.

Eventually, this rhythmic tick-tock of the heart chimes its reveille and we begin to ask the time-related questions we were created to ask. *Why am I here? What is my purpose? Is there a God?*

He has made everything beautiful in its time. Also He has put eternity in their hearts. (Ecclesiastes 3:11)

My grandparents have always been a big part of my life. I joke that they showed up an hour early and sat in the front row for everything. From dance recitals to school plays, they didn't miss a thing. My grandfather played the saxophone for his band, the Treble Makers, "blowing his horn," as he'd say, on weekends for the Italian clubs. When I hear songs such as "Spanish Eyes" or "It's Now or Never," I am transported to a family room in San Leandro, California, with brown shag rugs and gold beveled lamps, standing behind a microphone and singing at the top of my lungs.

When Grandma had us over to spend the night we would badger my grandfather until he set up his microphone and amplifier for me and my sisters. One weekend, Grandma compiled songs sung by my sisters and me on a cassette tape—a gift for my dad on Father's Day. I was taped singing Elvis Presley's version of "My Way."

"Let the record show I did it my way." Quite prophetic for a chatty little girl in the first grade. My life record shows from the age of seven until twenty-nine I did it my way. Little did I know my Redeemer was counting the seconds until our life together would begin.

When my spiritual alarm clock went off, I was in my bed. My mother had been battling cancer and I lay awake thinking of things I'd never allowed myself to think. The news of her second brain tumor earlier that day left me reeling. For the first time in more than a year of doctor's appointments and radiation therapy, I allowed myself to consider the horrible possibility of her death.

She could die. Could she really? What if she does? Then what? Will I ever see her again? Is there really a heaven? Will she go there? Will I go there?

"Paul, are you awake?" I whispered.

"No."

"You're not funny. I want to ask you something."

"What?"

"Do you believe in heaven?"

In the dark of night, like Nicodemus when he visited Jesus, I had the courage to ask my husband a difficult question. You see, I was the one who was supposed to have been raised to know God.

"Do you believe in heaven?" I asked again.

"Yes." He gently but firmly replied, his answer reverberating into the quiet darkness of our bedroom.

I have often said that my mom played a part in giving me life twice—first when I was born and second when I was born again. That evening, cloaked in the dark of night, her cancer set off eternity in my heart. Not long after that late-night conversation with my husband, I went to my knees in our home office and surrendered my life to Jesus.

Mom's death gave me a much greater appreciation of time. Death has the power to do that, at least temporarily. The real test is keeping the respect for time months after leaving the mortuary or funeral service. I don't believe anyone would choose to watch someone he or she loves die, but tears well up in my eyes, even now, when I recall all the ways God carried us during that difficult time.

Days before her death, she lay in a hospital bed in her family room. I'd followed my father back to their bedroom to ask him a question. I found him going through their dresser drawers, looking for something. With his back to me and unaware that I was there, he came across something and was holding it in his hands.

Feeling my presence, he turned toward me. That's when I saw it—one of my mother's silk nightgowns.

"The tags are still on this one." He smiled sadly.

My respect for time has lasted long past my mother's funeral. Her death was the life experience that gave me 20/20 eternal vision and shined a spotlight on what I was too busy and much too burdened about.

Only God knows when I will awaken to my last day. If I'm to live my life with purpose and wisdom, the Lord promises to redeem my time. Over the course of her two-year battle with cancer, through my mother's illness, I discovered ways I could do this. I've listed a few of my own personal time redeemers below.

- Every meal is the right time to use my china. My china plates sit on the bottom shelf in my kitchen, where my children have easy access to them. They will remember the pattern of tiny rosebuds beneath a bed of lettuce or slab of meatloaf. I think using my best plates for our everyday meals tells them they are special to me. While emptying our dishwasher this week, I noticed quite a few of my plates are now chipped and dull. They look used, and I couldn't help but smile.

- Pretty lingerie can be worn when it's not date night or an anniversary. I've made a point to wear every nightie I own. I may fall short when it comes to cleaning under the stove, but if the Lord takes me before Paul, I've made sure my husband will not come across anything in my dresser drawer with tags still attached.

- *I love you* and *I forgive you* are timeless words. While my mother was sick, we had time to share many *I love yous*. I make sure a day does not pass without blessing my family with those words. It surprised me when my girlfriend told me she had never heard these words from her mother. If this mom only knew how one *I love you* could redeem a lifetime of hurt.

* Toilet-papering your mother in a hospital bed is a great time redeemer.

Remodeling Time

My sister and I were visiting my mother. We had been told she had only weeks to live. Pulling up a stool, I was eye to eye with her. Confined to her hospital bed, she was now immobile. Seeing my once vibrant mother bedridden was painfully difficult. Cancer robbed her of so much, but she refused to let it steal her sense of humor.

Bringing my face right above hers, I gave her a wide, mischievous smile.

"What?" she asked nervously. Her mother's intuition told her I was up to something.

"I have a great idea."

"What?" she said impatiently.

I put my mouth by her ear and whispered, "I'm going to toilet-paper you."

Her head was stuck in one uncomfortable looking position, and she was in continual pain. Trying to use her angry mom-voice, she started to laugh. "Joanne, don't you dare!"

"Mom, save your breath, you can't do anything about it. I've waited years for this moment. What are you going to do, chase me?" I teased as I walked into the adjoining bathroom and hunted for a few rolls of toilet paper.

"Joooaaannne," she yelled as best as she could.

Walking back into the family room, I tossed my sister a roll and we got to work. As I weaved white tissue paper around the cold steel bed, Mom couldn't stop laughing. By the time we were done, her out-of-place hospital bed, that horrible reminder of her illness, looked like a float in the Macy's Thanksgiving Day Parade.

My sister made her a lovely white tissue hat, gently placing it on top of her head. The finishing touch was a bouquet of white tissue flowers that I put in her hands. We were laughing so hard there was no sound coming from any of us; my sister and I were bent over in pain from the stomach spasms of a good laugh.

An evening in which heartache reigned was remodeled into a beautiful memory for my sister and me. A painful moment in time was redeemed for all three of us that night.

Whether our life is picture perfect or being tossed in a sea of heartache, God has given us the ability to redeem time by using it intentionally.

**Ask Him to show you ways you can spend
His blessed currency with your family.**

Our radical sabbatical was a year-long lesson about His gift of time. When I surrendered my chaotic, topsy-turvy busyness into His hands on New Year's Day, He redeemed my time and opened my eyes to freedom from the captivity of my overactivity. I felt as if the Lord was saying, *A new year begins today, let's try something different. I'm going to fill your home with more hours to be a family.*

Don't forget, He created time. He is not bound by its rules. Who better to show us how to mold and shape it in our favor?

Dear Lord, teach me to number my days so I may gain a heart of wisdom. Help me treasure each new morning. Show me where I can work to make a life that shows my husband and children they are more important to me than my china. In Jesus' name I pray. Amen.

- Where would your loved ones leave notes if they wanted to be sure you would see them?
- Do you use your china? What about special jewelry or your fancy nightgown? If not, what are you waiting for?
- Call your mom and dad and tell them you love them today.

YOUR HOME IS A MEMORY MUSEUM

One time I went to a museum where all the work in the museum had been done by children. They had all the paintings up on refrigerators.

—*Stephen Wright*[1]

A tradition is a family custom, a unique fingerprint of your very own social DNA passed through the generations. Traditions brand hearts with your family name and are not exclusive to holidays.

A grand yearly vacation spot or something as small as a note tucked away in your child's lunch box can spark a family tradition. All are invaluable. I can almost hear Tevya in *Fiddler on the Roof*, dancing around singing about his love of "Tradition!" My heart is dancing right along with him. Tradition is the family business that churns out countless memories on its blessed assembly line.

Do you realize you own your very own museum? Your home is a Smithsonian of memories in the making. From your kitchen table to your family room sofa, each room holds memory-making potential. Within the insulated walls of your dwelling place, whether or not you are aware of it, you are making a museum of memories with your children.

The World's Largest Museum of Memories

The Smithsonian Institution is the world's largest museum complex. Made up of seventeen different museums, it displays everything from the Hope Diamond to the Wright Brothers' first plane. It is not humanly possible to see the Smithsonian in one day, and definitely not in ninety minutes, the time allotted our busload of eighth graders to stay on our tight sightseeing schedule.

This was the first trip to D.C. for me and my daughter Meghan. We knew this was a trip of a lifetime. Meghan had sold her weight in candy bars, and unless Paul and I won the Publisher's Clearinghouse Sweepstakes, we wouldn't be taking a future family trip there together.

As the bus came to a stop, we quickly made our plan. Meghan and I wanted to see every one of the seventeen museums. *What? We can only pick one?* It felt like a Smithsonian Sophie's Choice to me. If we had to choose only one, it would have to be the American History Museum. My daughter lived and breathed American history. I knew it was an easy decision for her. The moment we got off the bus we ran as fast as we could in the direction of the American History Museum.

Forgive me, I'm exaggerating here, I didn't run. Meghan ran. I was "munning." *Munning* is mom-running, a befuddled, waddle-gallop known to those of us with wider hips and smaller bladders.

It's important to keep in mind that my daughter Meghan is a history hound. She loves history. She loves it so much that on the third day of our trip, on hallowed Mount Vernon ground, she brought out the worst in me.

- Day 1: I beamed with mom-pride, thinking to myself, *Look at all she knows about the birth of our country. Everyone, listen to my daughter!*
- Day 2: *She knows more than the tour guide! Are you listening people? My daughter knows everything about our beautiful country!*
- Day 3: *Put a sock in it, Meghan. I'm sick of hearing all you know. Lord, save me from this child.*

While visiting Mount Vernon, we walked by the slave quarters. I admired the tiny houses with old-fashioned, wood-paned glass. Bending down, I peeked into one of the warped windows.

"Goodness these windows are old, aren't they, Honey? Can you imagine the families living inside each tiny house? Little faces stood up on tip-toe and peeked out of these windows at one time."

"Mom, these windows aren't original. Slaves weren't allowed to have windows in their houses."

"Of course, they were. Look at how old these are. You think you know everything sweetheart, but you really don't."

"I know slave quarters didn't have windows."

Right there on George Washington's property, her little Mom-I-know-so-much-more-than-you smirk set me off. Martha would have been irritated too if she'd seen the look she gave me.

"Excuse me, Mr. Tour Guide. Sir . . ." I bustled up to the front of our group, getting the attention of a gentleman so old I believe he might have known the first president personally.

"Yes, ma'am?"

"Are these wood-paned windows over here original to the slave quarters? My daughter believes they were added later."

Yes. I did it. I'm not ashamed of it either. After three incredibly long days, I picked up my history-loving daughter and threw her under the tour bus.

"Your daughter is absolutely correct. These windows are not original. They were added later. Wow, I've been a tour guide here for years and years, and no one has ever known that before."

Meghan puffed up with I-told-you-so pride, and I smiled a smile at the tour guide that only my daughter would recognize as foul.

That day, on our Founding Father's soil, my lack of knowledge may have crawled right under my skin, but a memory was created for my daughter. It would forever be the day her mother challenged her and she was crowned victorious.

Memories don't always have to start out well to finish well. Their staying power is in how you respond to them later. It's been six years, and we still look back on that memory and laugh. I believe we always will.

Scrapper or Picture-Taker?

If you were to walk down the hallway in our home, you'd discover thirty-three black-framed pictures hanging on my walls. I admit that I'm a little kooky when it comes to pictures. I don't scrapbook as much as I should—or as much as I wish I could. I'm a disorganized perfectionist. After a few hours, my creative juices are on empty and I can't find the scissors to save my scrapper-life.

"Everyone, come over and see what I just created. This is a flower. I've cut the petals so they can hold pictures of all of your heads inside. I'm going to make a whole scrapbook of flower-heads, this way you can open up a scrapbook each season to see what you were doing at the age of four." I beam, holding up a sunflower with the distorted head of my husband inside.

"But, Mom, I really don't care what I was doing at four," David mumbles, walking back to his bedroom.

"I don't want my head in a flower!" Samuel adds.

"Who is that?" Meghan asks, looking more closely.

"It's your father," I reply, annoyed.

"Dad would hate to be in a flower, Mom. He has allergies, remember?" Grace reminds me.

I may not be the world's best scrapbooker, but I do take my fair share of family pictures. As a matter of fact, I watched the first three years of my oldest daughter's life through the lens of a camera.

I've got boxes full of pictures shoved in numerous dark corners of my house. Walking down the main artery of our home, one is surrounded by a sea of black-framed photos. Memories greet us there daily. I change the pictures each season. So check the box next to obsessive-compulsive.

In the summer there are pictures of trips to the ocean, swim parties, and berry-picking excursions. Each day during fall, my family walks down our hallway to see their faces smiling back at them behind caramel apples, trips to pumpkin patches, and leaves aglow in burnt oranges and lipstick reds.

The kids enjoy seeing the pictures that change with each season. Our hallway is the record keeper of all kinds of memories. When we took our sabbatical, we made it a point to stay loyal to our family traditions, and we even picked up a few more to call our own.

Swim-Tuesdays

Swimming pools are not a luxury where I live; they are a necessity. Our summers are extremely hot. When we had our pool built we decided to set aside a day for friends and neighbors to come over for a swim.

Admittedly, this tradition is as much for moms as it is for kids.

We deemed that Tuesdays the backyard would be open for moms and their kids to take a dip and cool off from the heat. Over the years, I've enjoyed bringing out a pitcher of iced tea and visiting with moms who brought their little ones over. While our children splash and play in the pool, we share recipes, funny stories, and even a few tears. We've prayed together and laughed together as our children cooled off and burned off some summer energy.

Even our backyards have memory-making potential.

Annual Ditch-Day

Warning: If you are a schoolteacher, please stick your fingers in your ears through the next couple of paragraphs and repeat after me, "Lalalalalalalalalalalalalalalalala."

I'm not sure how this special day began in our home, but it did. My husband is none too crazy about its existence. It's probably the *professor* in him. But it's true that each year we let our kids ditch a day of school.

It is really more of a *controlled* annual ditch day. We don't let our children decide when the day is going to be. I don't plan for it or talk much about it at all really. It's kind of like a Big Foot holiday. It's something that's been heard to take place in our home, yet our children are too scared to ask us about it for fear they may not see it.

A ditch day in our home can happen in a variety of ways:

- I let them get up and get ready for school before I share the good news. This way they're showered and ready to take on our day's adventures together.
- I unplug their alarm clocks the night before so they oversleep. This way I get a good laugh when they exit their room the next morning all bedhead and crazy-eyed, like a clown shot from a circus cannon.
- I tell them the night before, giving them Christmas Eve joy as they jump into bed wondering what the next day will bring.
- I've even picked up my high schoolers in the morning from school. I let them attend the first-period class before surprising them and taking them out for the rest of the day.

Ditch days can only be experienced one child at a time. In the past, I have taken both girls together, scrapbooking, playing dress-up in my old prom dresses, and putting make-up on each other. It was a sweet time. But I still think having one-on-one time is best for a ditch day if you can swing it.

A friend recently shared how her teenage daughter was running for junior high school president. I learned later her little girl lost the election and was crushed. I suggested she pick her up from school and share a ditch day together. She loved the idea.

My children aren't studying medicine at Harvard, so I've been able to squelch the mom-guilt. And if I plan things well, our time together becomes a day to treat my child to a matinee, grab a dollar value meal together, and spend special time with the child I love. Ditch days have been one of our kids' favorite memory makers. I'm sure you're not surprised.

Teachers: You can take your fingers out of your ears now.

Our Thanksgiving Tablecloth[2]

When I was a little girl, Thanksgiving dinners were at my grandparent's house. My grandpa was Italian, and it was our family tradition to have pasta with our turkey dinner, Christmas dinner, birthday dinner, Fourth of July barbecues, and any other meal shared at their table. I can't look at a bowl of mostaccioli without thinking of my grandpa.

Traditions don't have to be big productions or make big dents in your bank account. Some of our personal favorites have begun without us even trying. We decorate our Christmas tree while eating Rice Krispies treats and drinking hot cocoa. We annually attend free museum day in Sacramento on the first Saturday in February, just to name a couple. But our favorite family tradition by far is our Thanksgiving tablecloth.

Our special custom began in November 2001. I was hosting our family turkey day only weeks after 9/11. Like all Americans, we were licking our wounds from our hurts and thinking of so many whose Thanksgiving dinners would never be the same.

As soon as we finished our meal, out came the ceremonial fabric pens. All who gathered around our table were encouraged to take turns writing on the tablecloth what they were thankful for. Our favorite family tradition was born that day.

As the years have passed, this linen tablecloth has become precious to me. Notes of gratitude for spouses, children, our country, and our God dance across the pale yellow cloth. Each small child has had his or her hands outlined by Mommy or Daddy, while Great Grandma Cusumano's shaky signature holds its rightful place in the very center of our table.

Now each November my children request the honor of putting out the tablecloth, just as they request to put the angel on top of our Christmas tree or candles on their birthday cakes. When Thanksgiving arrives, company gathers around our table hours before the turkey and stuffing make their grand entrance. Guests laugh at the memories while young children search to find their handprints, thrilled to see how much they've grown.

Once our guests are gone and the dishes have been put away, it's time for a personal tradition of my own, reading in solitude the special messages left behind by my family and friends. They may not be present for every turkey dinner, but their words remain on the cloth, hugging my heart, and reminding me to offer up a prayer of thanksgiving for every one of them.

Dear Lord, thank you for family traditions. I desire to create a museum of God-honoring and joy-filled memories in our home. Give me a creative mind to think of ways I can carve out time in my week to spend alone with each of my children. Grow us together through both the good and the sometimes not-so-good moments. In Jesus' name I pray. Amen.

- Have a family meeting. Come up with new family traditions together.
- Time spent on our children is an investment that brings a wealth of dividends. Write down a list of things you'd like to do with your child. Try and mark off one a week.
- Ideas for great memory-makers: Hike and bring along a picnic lunch. If it's raining, eat your picnic lunch by the fireplace. Take your bikes to a trail you haven't explored before. Have a coloring contest. Find a local park and lie on a blanket and read books together, or share a deli sandwich and watch the clouds pass by.

LEGACY LIVING

20

Life is a short and fevered rehearsal of a concert we cannot stay to give.

—*A. W. Tozer*[1]

Every president of the United States desires it and parents underestimate it—their legacies for future generations.

Parenting is a living legacy, an unseen organism, alive and growing this very moment. Time is the tool used to mold and form a legacy into something of beauty. I didn't think about it much when I was a child. It wasn't on my mind as a young adult when I moved out of my parents' home. But, in time, in the same way I discovered my first gray hair or the moment I realized *I really do love brussels sprouts*, I made a conscious decision to work on my legacy as a mom.

A legacy is something I get to leave behind when I'm gone. For visiting guests, my legacy might be kind words or a fun-filled evening. A teacher's legacy is a future of adults who remember times tables and the capital of Kentucky. A pastor's legacy is a congregation that matures and grows in the knowledge of Jesus Christ to become His hands and feet in a hurting world.

As a mom, my legacy is all of the above and more, formed over seconds, minutes, days, and years.

Our radical sabbatical became the
blank canvas of our parenting legacy.

Legacy hours aren't exclusive to Monday through Friday 8 A.M. to 3 P.M. or on Sunday mornings. Day in and day out, sun up to sun down, my children are watching me closely to learn what exactly it is I hold dear and how I apply these truths to my life.

As a writer, I leave my mark on the world with my words. Stacks of journals litter our bonus room closet. I've kept them in the hopes a child or grandchild may one day step into my life. My thoughts and dreams swirling on the pages might draw them in, uncovering the treasures of my heart. My words on paper are the fingerprint left behind to remind my family I was here.

From their great-grandma's rice pudding recipe, the one she makes every time I visit her, to the words I recently heard my grown-up child say that sounded just like me, I have a chance each day to leave my kids with tiny pieces of me.

When my oldest daughter decided she wanted to move out of our home, she was not yet eighteen. She had graduated high school months before, and while she completed her undergraduate degree at our local junior college, she had to get out from under our roof or she would just die. I couldn't blame her. I'd felt the very same way when I was her age.

When my children were young I had a keen awareness of how temporarily they would all be under my roof. I would creep into their bedrooms and stand beside them to watch them sleep. I'd search for the rise and fall of their dream-filled breaths and thank God for giving me such precious gifts. Now, my oldest chickadee wanted to spread her wings and fly my coop. I shed quite a few tears the two weeks before she left. I kept them from her because encouragement was the constant I wanted her to feel from me.

I was concerned about her being on her own. *What if she stayed out too late? What if she didn't eat well? What if she got a flat tire on*

181

the freeway—at night? What-ifs ran amuck in my mind, followed by self-centered concerns about my mom-legacy. This was it. Her time under my constant care was ending. Sure, she'd be home to visit and pop over from time to time to do her laundry or raid the refrigerator of ice cream and a home-cooked meal. But the years God had given her to me, to keep her safely nestled under my soft, downy mama wings was coming to an end.

It's Never Too Late to Change Our Parenting Legacy

A legacy is a living thing. I had to remind myself when Meghan moved out that being a mom wasn't over.

My legacy is alive. It's been growing and developing from the moment I took my first legacy-mom breath in the delivery room and won't finish expanding and growing until the day I die.

A parenting legacy is the most beautiful of all legacies and has the longest reach through the generations. Sadly, I believe it's the one most frequently given up on.

All parents make mistakes. We're human. I remember sharing with my friend Mary, "I'm not going to make the same mistakes my parents made."

She quickly replied, "No, you won't make the same mistakes. You'll make different ones."

My father wrote a letter to me one Christmas when my children were young. In it he spoke of his love for me and his pride in having been a part of watching me grow up. He went on to share his heart of regret over being too rough on me. He was not abusive, but he was definitely strict. One Marine plus one hard-headed teenage daughter equaled quite a few colorful family moments. I was his oldest child, which meant I was his first recruit.

As a young girl, I received the discipline of a soldier who saw only black and white. As a teenager, I didn't like it one bit. As an adult, I am grateful. "Dad, you don't need to apologize. I turned out the best of all your children," I like to joke.

My father's letter is dear to me. I keep it in the same box as my Christmas Nativity, so I get to read it every time I put out our holiday decorations. Concerned about his legacy as my dad, in his letter he tries to right the wrongs. I love him for that. I'm not sure if he realizes his legacy of being "too strict" has grown into a legacy of a loving father who desires to encourage and love his child, no matter what her age.

Joey, your mom and I have done the best we can. We have loved you and raised you to know the Lord. We have also made a few mistakes along the way. You are a grown woman now, with babies of your own, and you can't use our mistakes as excuses. Take and use those things from us that are good, that we did right, and leave the rest behind.

Unfortunately, there are mistakes that can scar a child. I've discovered over the years that parents who've left the deepest scars are often the ones who concede most quickly to legacy's defeat. When their children are grown and bring up the past, or when their adult kids openly work on forgiving their parents, these moms and dads lose hope their legacy will ever be anything more. Sins of their parenting past stunt their legacy, holding it in a still, dark place.

At a women's conference this summer, Julia shared about being raised by an abusive father. She told a story of abuse and heartache. She'd served for years on a worship team and was always so upbeat, so tender and kind. How could this be any part of her story? As surprised as I was to hear of her victimization, what surprised me even more was her abundant joy.

"I have forgiven my father. And today we are able to have a relationship."

Julia's joy came from the deep well of forgiveness. She had let go of the right she had to hurt her father and forgave him instead. Julia lives each day with joy. The heartache and hurt of her childhood are between her father and God now.

What Will Your Parenting Legacy Be?

I love people. There isn't anywhere I go I don't hope to meet or talk to someone new. I want to hear about them, their children, their spouses, their joys, their heartaches, their stories. I would love to pick out strangers' names in the phonebook and interview them, or even stop by their homes and spend an afternoon with them. As a Christian, I believe there should be a television station devoted to testimonies. I would hook up our cable again for such a station.

As much as I love to meet living, breathing people—call me odd—but old cemeteries call to me. If we're out for a drive and happen to see one, I make my husband stop. We enjoy walking around and reading the gravestones. Who were these people? What did they hold dear? Whose lives did they touch? What's their story?

David was six when we stepped past the rusty iron gates and into a local gold-rush cemetery in the shade of gnarled oak trees. Immediately, our son ran off in a different direction to explore on his own.

"Dad! Come quick!" His scream made us jump. Paul and I ran to where our son was standing and pointing.

He was almost beside himself, anxiously hopping from one foot to the other. "It says, 'I'm not dead. I'm just sleeping.' Dad, she's not dead! She's just sleeping!" His eyes pleaded with his father to do something. To prevent our son from getting down on his hands and knees and digging, our little boy had to be schooled on the tombstone definition of *sleeping*.

We have pretty dark senses of humor, my husband and I. That probably is a result of our police backgrounds; we secretly laughed about it later when David wasn't around.

While at a marriage conference, the speaker passed out pieces of paper to everyone in the audience. On it was the gray outline of a tombstone. The speaker challenged us to write our own epitaph.

My husband and I were stumped. *What would we write? How would we be remembered? What did we want our legacy to be?* Paul began to write, "I'm not dead. I'm sleeping."

"You're not funny," I whispered.

I like what Erma Bombeck requested on her gravestone. "Big deal! I'm used to dust."[2]

My mom told me before she died she wanted hers to read, "I told you I was sick." My father decided to stick with the traditional tombstone lingo when she passed. I'm expecting to have to answer for that one day.

I was reminded that I'm not the one who will choose the words on my grave marker, nor will I get to put together the words shared at my funeral service. With four children, there will be four opportunities to speak publicly on my behalf. *What will they say?* My legacy will be laid bare for all to see, the good, the bad, and the ugly. My children will finally have the last word.

There's a tiny newspaper clipping I cut out years ago and placed between the pages of my journal. Yellowed with age, it is an obituary. I don't know this woman. I've never met her before in my life. But when I read the legacy she left behind, the few words her family chose to share with the world about her, I was touched. I was so touched that I cut it out of our local newspaper and slipped it inside my journal. I remember thinking as I cut it out, *This is what I want my legacy to be.*

Jane Margaret Hunter

Jane Margaret Hunter, 69 yrs., passed away April 3 at her Placerville residence. She was born October 26, 1934 in Moline, Kansas.

After the usual statistics of her name, age, when she died, and where she was from, it said:

Proverbs 31:10-31, Virtuous Wife

Mom, we your children rise up and call you blessed, your husband also and he praises you.

A gift to her family and anyone whose path crossed hers, she left her footprints on our hearts. Such an inspiration with her creative abilities, her home was more than a place to live, truly a home for all who entered.

A woman of great faith, this inheritance was the most important for her to pass down to the generations as well as to her siblings. Even in her greatest trials, she put others before herself, praying for them on behalf of their families.

A godly legacy doesn't just happen. It is knowingly, prayerfully, and painstakingly created. I used to believe the busier I was the greater my legacy. Have you considered what yours will be?

My legacy casts a shadow on all I do as a mom. We are born with a deeply rooted desire to be remembered. I can tell you this much, I know how I don't want to be remembered.

I don't want my children to have mental snapshots of me racing back and forth from one busy moment to another. I don't want them to remember a childhood with me squawking about each misplaced shin-guard or firing cheeseburgers into the backseat of the car as we rush to the next soccer practice. If activities ever again take up all our family time or stand in the way of my godly legacy, they will have to be considered for the chopping block.

I will battle busyness for the rest of my life. I'm eternally grateful for our radical sabbatical and for the twelve months we experienced as we slowed down together.

Have you considered taking your own radical sabbatical yet?

It doesn't have to be just like ours. Your family is unique. There are many ways you can come up for air and take a breath from a busy schedule. If you aren't able to take a year-long activity time out, how about taking a sabbatical from fast food and eat sitting down around your kitchen table?

Remember: when friends tell you a radical sabbatical is nutty, if they laugh and point, remind them you refuse to be in bondage to your busyness or in captivity to your activities. You are using your gift of time wisely, and your legacy will reflect that.

After visiting a church to hear a new preacher in town, President Abraham Lincoln is reported to have said of the sermon, "It was good, but he didn't ask me to do anything great."[3] Abraham Lincoln wanted to be challenged. He wanted something to reach for. And that's what God asks of us.

And, sometimes, what God asks of us looks a little bit radical.

ENDNOTES

Chapter 1
1. Barbara Johnson, *Stick a Geranium in Your Hat and Be Happy* (Nashville: Thomas Nelson, 2004).
2. Lays Chips advertisement, Keeping Up with the Joneses, in *Better Homes and Gardens* (July 2008).
3. *100 Days of Prayer for Women* (Grand Rapids, Mich.: Family Christian Stores, 2008), 25.

Chapter 2
1. Bill Watterson quote, http://www.billwatterson.net/more.html.
2. Linda Sparrowe, "Addicted to Stress?" *Natural Health* (July-August 2010).
3. *100 Days of Prayer for Women*, 67.

Chapter 3
1. Billy Graham, "How Do We Help the Hurting?" Available at http://www .billygraham.org/articlepage.asp?articleid=238 (October 1, 2002).
2. Joanne Kraft, "See Jane Run," *Proverbs 31 Woman Magazine* (March 2009).
3. Bruce Bickel and Stan Jantz, *God Is in the Small Stuff—for Your Family* (Uhrichsville, Ohio: Barbour, 1999).

Chapter 4
1. Ellen Goodman, "Our Time-Crunch Disorder," *Boston Globe* (March 27, 2005).
2. Ellie Lofaro, *Leap of Faith* (Colorado Springs: Cook Communications, 2004).
3. *100 Days of Prayer for Women*, 219.
4. Ibid., 126.

Chapter 5
1. Karen O'Connor, *Squeeze the Moment: Making the Most Out of Life's Gifts and Challenges* (Ventura, Calif.: Regal Books, 2005).

Chapter 6
1. Jean Cherni, "Simply Put, a Little Planning Reduces Your Grocery Bill," *New Haven Register* (October 27, 2010).
2. Ruth Bell Graham, *It's My Turn* (Old Tappan, N.J.: Fleming H. Revell, 1982).

Chapter 7
1. Erma Bombeck, *A Marriage Made in Heaven . . . Or Too Tired for an Affair* (New York: Harper Collins, 1993).
2. Joanne Kraft, "Why Animals Eat Their Young," *Light from the Word, Vista Magazine* (September 2010).

Chapter 8

1. Robert and Debbie Morris, *The Blessed Marriage* (Southlake, Tex.: Gateway Church, 2006).

2. "Blessed is the nation whose God is the Lord, the people He has chosen as His own inheritance."

3. Joanne Kraft, "What Hills Are You Dying On?" *Christianity Today-Kyria Magazine; Marriage Partnership Magazine* (January 2011).

4. Johnson, *Stick a Geranium in Your Hat and Be Happy.*

Chapter 9

1. Todd Hertz, "Deliver Us from Evil," *Christianity Today*, http://www.christianity today.com/iyf/hottopics/faithvalues/31.50.html.

2. Anthony DiChiara, "Prepared to Be Scared all over Again," *The Examiner* (September 16, 2010).

3. Beth Moore, *A Quick Word with Beth Moore: Scriptures and Quotations from Breaking Free* (Nashville: B&H Publishing Group, 2008).

Chapter 10

1. *100 Days of Prayer for Women*, 259.

2. Ibid.

Chapter 11

1. Jean Tracy, "3 Parenting Tips for Handling Peer Pressure," Go Articles (October 31, 2007).

Chapter 12

1. Karen Deerwester, *The Entitlement-Free Child* (Naperville, Ill.: Sourcebooks, 2007).

Chapter 13

1. Quoted in Danny Britton and Jimmy Page, *Wisdom Walks* (Minneapolis: Summerside, 2010).

2. Becky Tirabassi, *Let Prayer Change Your Life* (Nashville: Thomas Nelson, 1999).

3. Graham, *It's My Turn.*

4. *More Joy for the Journey: A Woman's Secret to a Balanced Life* (Nashville: Thomas Nelson, 2007).

Chapter 14

1. Ted Goodman, *The Forbes Book of Business Quotations: 10,000 Thoughts on the Business of Life* (New York: Black Dog and Leventhal, 1997).

Chapter 16

1. Elizabeth Bernstein, "Your BlackBerry or Your Wife," *Wall Street Journal*, http://online.wsj.com/article/SB10001424052748703779704576073801833991620. html.

2. "Unplug Your Kids," *Good Housekeeping* (November 2010), 107.

3. Cheryl Pawlowski, *Glued to the Tube* (Naperville, Ill.: Sourcebooks, 2000).
4. Ibid.
5. A Kaiser Family Foundation Study, "Generation M2: Media in the Lives of 8- to 18-Year-Olds," http://www.kff.org/entmedia/ (January 2010).
6. Ibid.

Chapter 17
1. Joanne Kraft, "Recollection Road," *Proverbs 31 Woman Magazine* (April 2010), 10-11.

Chapter 18
1. *A Dictionary of Hymnology* (New York: Charles Scribner and Sons, 1892).

Chapter 19
1. Stephen Wright, "Stephen Wright Quotes." Available at http://laughnet.net/ (October 27, 2010).
2. Joanne Kraft, "The Thanksgiving Tablecloth," *ParentLife Magazine* (October 2009).

Chapter 20
1. Ellen Santilli Vaughn, *Time Peace* (Grand Rapids, Mich.: Zondervan, 2007).
2. *Age Happens* (New York: Meadowbrook Press, 1996).
3. Jill Briscoe, *Spiritual Arts: Mastering the Disciplines for a Rich Spiritual Life* (Grand Rapids, Mich.: Zondervan, 2010).

Grace & Truth Living

Strengthening Families Through the Love of Christ

Paul & Joanne Kraft believe in strengthening families through the love of Christ. They would love the opportunity to share with your church, Bible study, or MOPS group. To contact one or both for your future speaking engagement—stop by Grace & Truth Living.
www.GraceandTruthLiving.com

Share *Just Too Busy* with your women's study, MOPS group, or summer book club. Inspire your friends to tame time-stealers, break free from the captivity of over-activity, and redeem the gift of time with their families. Download the group leader study guide today <www.JoanneKraft.com>.

And the Word became flesh and dwelt among us,
and we beheld His glory, the glory as of
the only begotten of the Father,
full of grace and truth.
John 1:14